Continuous Line Quilting Designs

ESPECIALLY FOR MACHINE QUILTING

Pat Cody

CHILTON BOOK COMPANY   RADNOR, PENNSYLVANIA

For a True Craftsman
This book was made possible by a grant from
Jerry R. Pierce.

Where Credit Is Due . . .
Production art was prepared by Arlene Talladino
with her usual flair, on top of her full-time art
director's job.

"Lightning Strikes Thrice," "Iristocrat," and
"Turning Over New Leaves" were first published in
Needle & Thread magazine. "Starry Nights" was
first published in *Country Handcrafts* magazine.

All quilted items shown were designed and made
by the author.

Copyright © 1984 by Pat Cody
All Rights Reserved
Published in Radnor, Pennsylvania 19089 by Chilton Book Company
Designed by Jean Callan King/Metier Industrial, Inc.
Manufactured in the United States of America

Library of Congress Cataloging in Publication Data
Cody, Pat, 1943-
    Continuous line quilting designs.
    1. Machine quilting—Patterns.   I. Title.
TT835.C63 1984   746.46′041   83-45385
ISBN 0-8019-7453-4 (pbk.)

1 2 3 4 5 6 7 8 9 0   3 2 1 0 9 8 7 6 5 4

Contents

Introduction

A quilt without piecing is a whole-cloth quilt, but a pieced top without quilting is unfinished. Those vital stitches that lock top, batting, and backing together can also be a design feature for machine quilters with continuous line designs.

Few hand-quilting designs can be machine-stitched; they're full of short lines, gaps, and convoluted swirls. Machine-quilting designs continue for long distances, with few start-stops where threads are fastened. Designs flow in unbroken lines, allowing for the range of fabric movement that is possible with a machine.

Machine quilting is a valuable addition to your repertoire of techniques and is especially suited to certain purposes. (1) When fabric is difficult or impossible to hand quilt, your machine gives you the go-ahead. (2) When quilted items get heavy use and frequent washings, machine quilting can provide durability. (Two threads are stronger than one.) (3) Machine-stitched lines are more visible, causing greater loft with thinner batting and making a stronger design statement. (4) Machine quilting is faster than hand quilting, so you bring alive more ideas in the same time.

You won't need a special machine to reproduce these designs. My own projects are quilted on two home-model Singers that are about the age of rock 'n' roll music.

I recommend *The Complete Book of Machine Quilting* by the Fannings as a helper (see Shopping Center). This book gives far more information than a design book can provide.

Getting to Know This Book

Look through the design pages as you read to get well acquainted with this book. Designs are printed against a ¼-inch *grid* to help you resize them. Design lines go from one grid intersection to another—a specific number of blocks away—before they change. I call those points of change *turning points.*

On each design page, you'll find a bracket labeled *repeat unit*; this identifies a segment of the design. Reproduce it again and again, hooking one unit onto the next, to extend the design.

You'll also see that designs are drawn with lines that look different: solid, dashed, dotted, and dash-dotted lines. Each line depicts a separate *quilting path.* You sew one path at a time, sewing return trips when paths intersect at row ends.

When designs have several paths, look first at the repeat unit. Follow each different line separately with your finger to get a feel for its movement. Often a design's bottom half is a mirror image of the top half.

As you become familiar with these designs, you will become more confident. By the time you've resized or made stencils, marked designs onto your projects, and stitched samples, you'll know every path in a design as well as the way to your favorite fabric store.

Each design in this book carries size information under its title. These measurements tell you the height and the width of the repeat unit to help you plan its use. Along with each design there is a helpful hint about marking or stitching or a project idea for using the pattern.

All border designs show a way to turn corners. Just rotate the corner turn to make the other three corners you need.

If a design faces a definite direction, as in "Birkie Scots," an about-face is easy. Trace the design as is, turn the tracing over, and retrace it on the back of the same paper.

Rows of border designs make overall designs, bringing out another motif in the spaces between them. Connect row ends within designs so you stitch a return trip without start-stops. You can also connect row ends to the next row, alternating sides, so you quilt a line over the whole project.

Quilting as a Design Tool

If all quilting lines on a project are about the same shape and distance apart, the results may be boring. Combine designs so there's some variety of puffed shapes and areas where quilted lines vary in closeness. Decide whether to lead eyes vertically or horizontally as you plan quilted rows.

A simple design, such as "Fold, Spindle," has less variety within itself than does a more complex pattern, such as "Diamonds in the Rough." When you can use several designs on projects, choose only one as busy as "Diamonds." An overall design like "Taking the Floor" or simple designs like "Perforate" are good companions to a busy pattern.

All-straight lines give a feeling of energetic movement, like marching; all-curved lines feel more graceful, like waltzing. Your projects can combine both feelings, but let one dominate (as roasted nuts accent, not overpower, sweet brownies).

Fitting Designs on Projects

The most important part of putting these designs on projects is using your own two Is: imagination and individuality. Like other quilting tools, these designs come to life only when you use them to express your own tastes and judgment.

When you've chosen a quilting design and size for a block, test the pattern before stitching. Draw the design on see-through tracing paper and lay it over the block. Do quilting lines fall attractively over pieced areas? Are stitching lines close enough to secure the batting you've chosen?

Quilting take-up is a planning consideration when a finished project must fit a body or a bed. Quilting shrinks original dimensions, and usually the more quilting, the more take-up. A general rule is to allow 1 extra inch for every 8 project inches to compensate for quilting take-up.

For quilted clothing, you may cut pieces at least 2 inches larger all around, quilt them, and then cut to fit pattern pieces exactly. A good resource book on quilted clothing is Jean Ray Laury's *Quilted Clothing* (see Shopping Center).

Resizing Designs

You'll often use designs just as shown, but at times you'll want to resize them. Like any quilting technique, resizing looks hard only until you know how to do it.

The "connect-the-dots" method takes little equipment. First, look at a repeat unit of the design. Make dots at every turning point, where quilting paths change direction. Count how many blocks wide and tall the repeat unit is.

On another paper, mark off an area the size you want for the new repeat unit. Divide the width and height of the new area into the same number of blocks as in the book, making the blocks equal in size. Now transfer each dot on the grid in the book to your new grid.

When design lines are straight between dots, connect them using a ruler. When design lines curve, make more dots between turning points on each grid line the curved line touches. Connect dots with short, light pencil lines. (Pretend your pencil is a feather duster, not a scrub brush.) Compare your drawing with the original, erasing and resketching until you're satisfied. Trace your new repeat unit as many times as you want for your stencil. With practice, this method becomes child's play.

Mead makes a desk blotter pad of graph paper measuring 17 by 22 inches, handy for enlargements. Check for it at office supply stores.

To learn more about resizing designs, get Rita Weiss' book *The Artist's and Craftsman's Guide to Reducing, Enlarging and Transferring Designs* (see Shopping Center).

Making Stencils

Tracing a drawing is one of the simplest methods for getting designs off paper and onto fabric. If you have a glass-topped table, set an unshaded lamp under it. You can also put a drop light into a cardboard box and lay a sheet of rigid plastic over the top, making an inexpensive light box. Tape the drawing onto the table top or plastic box cover, turn on the light, position fabric onto the drawing, and trace. You'll find drawings easier to see through fabrics if you darken lines with a black felt-tipped pen.

Outline stencils work for single-line designs, such

as "Triple Crown." Draw the stitching lines onto plastic, cut out the shape, and you're ready to draw around the stencil. This device is easy to make and enables you to see exactly where you're marking. (See Shopping Center for stencil supplies).

Cut-slot stencils are permanent and simple to use (Fig. 1). With a permanent-ink or film marker, trace the design onto plastic. Alternate bridges with marking slots along lines. Put plastic on an old magazine or the wrong side of a rotary cutter mat. Using a craft knife with a replaceable blade, cut closely along both sides of marked lines, leaving supporting bridges uncut. You may have to repeat cuts to break through. Keep fingers out of cutting paths, because knives slip easily.

You'll find double-bladed knives on the market; these cut both sides of marked lines at once. Choose one with blades fixed in the handle; others spread unevenly as you bear down. If I make initial cuts with the double blade, I use a single-bladed knife to cut through completely. This method is time-consuming; plan a couple of hours to make most stencils. You may feel wrist fatigue for a day or so afterward.

Melted-slot stencils are similar to cut-slot ones but are made with an electric pen rather than a knife. A stencil kit, similar to a woodburning kit, comes with start-up supplies. Begin by tracing the design onto plastic, leaving supporting bridges. Then trace lines with the heated pen, following kit cautions and instructions. The slot produced by the pen isn't wide enough to accommodate all markers easily, so I often widen slots with sharp-pointed scissors.

Write the repeat unit size on each stencil for future reference. Leave margins measuring at least $\frac{1}{2}$ inch on all stencil sides for strength. Make stencil edges straight and mark them in inches to help position them. If your stencils are like mine, they'll look ragged, but since lines even out in stitching, your finished project will look fine.

Choosing Fabric Markers

The most important thing to remember about markers (to paraphrase a common ad slogan) is,

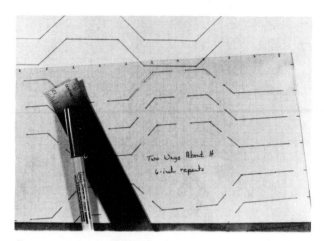

Figure 1. As you trace designs onto plastic, leave bridges along design lines for stronger stencils. Don't cut or melt through supporting bridges.

"try before you cry." The only safe marker for a fabric is one you've personally tested on that fabric.

Test markers and fabrics by prewashing. If a fabric is going to shrink, bleed, or otherwise misbehave, wouldn't you rather know it before investing time and effort? Fabrics can be machine-stitched more easily with sizing washed out, too.

Along one edge, mark a 6-inch line with a marker you might use. Follow the marker manufacturer's instructions for removing the line. Launder normally to be sure marks don't return after washing and drying. Different situations require different markers, so start a collection for use with various projects (see Shopping Center).

Several brands of felt-tipped water-erasable pens that make turquoise lines are sold. Follow the manufacturer's instructions and never press or use any chemical on fabrics with these marks on them. Heat, detergents, fabric glues, and fray deterrents can permanently set marks.

A soft-lead pencil meant to rinse out of fabric with cold water is the Dixon Washout Cloth Marker. Its red, blue, or green markings lighten but stay on fabrics during handling. The pencils are larger in diameter than ordinary pencils, so use a make-up pencil sharpener and keep leads short to avoid breaks.

Put white lines on dark fabrics with the Nonce Dark Fabric Marker. This soft-lead pencil needs only light marking pressure, and it's made to sponge out with water.

Soapstone zips around cut-out stencils and is available in a pencil form that can be sharpened for use with slotted stencils. Soapstone marks are visible on dark fabrics and usually rinse out.

Choosing Machine Quilting Materials

Machine quilting shows best on solid fabrics, a little on sparsely covered and two-color prints, and hardly at all on busy prints. You're free to quilt any material you can sew on your machine.

To select thread, I use the "birds of a feather" principle: Match the fiber content of the thread to that of the fabric when possible; at least you should use natural fibers together and man-made fibers together. The fabric must be stronger than the thread. You can restitch broken sewing lines more easily than you can repair thread-cut fabric. Be sure that thread used with washable fabric is also washable.

Presser-foot quilting is best done with threads you'd use to construct garments of the fabric. For free-machine quilting, enjoy the luster and brilance of machine embroidery threads.

Machines can stitch unusual batting materials, such as foam, down, blankets, fleece, and flannel. Bonded polyester batting is surface-treated to handle easily, stay lofty, and stand up to repeated washings. It's less likely to "beard," or peek through the surface of the fabric.

Bonded battings allow you to space quilting lines 4 to 6 inches apart. Unbonded polyester should be quilted every 3 inches; cotton should be quilted every 2 inches. With woven battings, such as sheet blankets, space quilting lines as you choose. As in hand quilting, the higher the loft of the batting, the more experienced the quilter must be.

Basting for Machine Quilting

Backing must be smooth and taut, but not stretched, before basting in order to prevent puckering. Assemble quilts in hand-quilting frames, or attach backing to a hard surface with masking tape before assembly with batting and top.

Projects may be thread- or pin-basted for machine quilting. Thread bastings hold work more securely, but bastings can catch in stitching and must be removed cautiously. Thread basting should be done in a 7- to 8-inch grid.

Pin basting is faster than thread basting, and, at 6- to 7-inch intervals, pins hold layers well. Safety pins will not stick you as much as straight pins will, since you tuck the points away. Use steel pins to avoid rust marks; you should invest in 200 to 300 pins to secure entire quilts.

Machine Quilting in General

We're the "right-now" generation of instant coffee, instant cameras, quick check-out lanes, and fast food chains. This attitude can lead to unrealistic expectations of machine quilting, which is never instant quilting. Speed depends on your own skills and standards. Generally, however, a machine-stitched quilt takes weeks, and a hand-stitched quilt takes months.

It is important to understand and care for your main tool, your machine. Know every opening that needs oil and every crevice where fuzz collects. Study your owner's manual and take lessons with local dealers.

Start quilting projects by cleaning and oiling your machine and putting in a new needle. Wind several bobbins at once for large projects. Then make a habit of brushing lint from the shuttle area every time you put in a new bobbin. Always quilt a sample "sandwich" of project materials to test machine settings, materials, and quilting method.

Stitching whole quilts in one piece is a bit cumbersome. Another approach is to segment projects into more manageable pieces (such as fronts, backs, and sleeves for garments). Quilts may be stitched in sections no more than 3 feet square or in border sections no more than 2 feet wide. This quilt-as-you-go approach lets you construct quilts in quarters or stitch medallions separately from borders before assembly.

Figure 2. Set a supporting surface behind your machine when quilting large projects like this quilt border. When projects hang off the machine, as the front part does here, the needle is pulled out of place. Thread-bastings hold these layers together.

Set a card table, or a similar surface, behind your machine to support items larger than 2 feet square. When the excess material is toward you, support it on your shoulder. The weight of unsupported quilting drags the needle out of position, causing uneven stitching and broken needles and thread (Fig. 2).

Since you sit at your machine for hours, protect your back. Sit erect in front of the needle, spine straight. Lean forward from the hips, resting your forearms on the machine. Hands go on either side of the needle, guiding fabric and holding it flat against the needle plate. You may want to spread the fingers of one hand in a V around the needle for better stitch-by-stitch control (Fig. 3).

Control is easier if you roll large projects on either side of the needle like a scroll, so just the path you're stitching shows. Secure rolls with large office clips, clothespins, or safety pins (Fig. 4).

Fasten threads securely at start-stops so quilting stays in your work. Try several methods and see which you prefer: (1) Backstitch four stitches at start-stops. (2) Pull front threads to the back and tie knots. (3) Pull front threads to the back, thread both on a hand needle, and weave into batting. (4) Make several stitches in one place to lock threads and trim closely.

Stitch slowly and evenly, never pushing or pulling work under the needle. Always stop with the needle down into the work, holding it in place like a third hand.

Special machine feet make certain quilting tasks easier. A walking foot moves all layers under the needle at the same rate, avoiding puckers and joining pieces evenly. An open-toed quilting or appliqué foot lets you see marked lines at the needle better. An embroidery or darning foot moves up and down with the needle, holding fabric against the needle plate and accommodating heavier thread layers of embroidered quilting (see Fig. 3).

Presser-Foot or Free-Machine Quilting?

Presser-foot quilting, like regular machine sewing, is done with the presser foot on. Free-machine quilting, like free-motion embroidery, is done without a presser foot, so you can move work in any direction.

Design size may suggest presser-foot or free-machine quilting; even very sharp curves in a 3-inch border may become gradual when sized for a 12-inch block. Generally, small design sizes, sharp turns, and short lines between turns mean it's easier to free-machine quilt.

Machine settings are simple for presser-foot quilting. You'll be straight-stitching, so the stitch width is 0. Choose a stitch length of 10 to 12 stitches per inch. You may need to loosen both top and bottom tensions, keeping them balanced; your sample "sandwich" will tell you. Use a small-hole needle plate to prevent jamming.

You can use presser-foot quilting more efficiently by practicing "quick turns." Stop at turning points with the needle in the work. Lift the presser bar lever with one hand, just enough to free the work, while the other hand turns it to its new position. Let the presser foot down again and stitch on.

For free-machine quilting, look at your owner's manual and follow the instructions for free-machine embroidery. Generally, both the stitch length and the width are set on 0. Loosen the top tension, but leave the bobbin tension at its normal setting. Put on a darning or an embroidery foot

Figure 3. Hands on either side of the needle help hold fabric against the needle plate, especially important for free-machine quilting. When you spread fingers around the needle, stitch cautiously to avoid catching them.

and lower the feed dogs, cover them, or raise the needle plate, whichever your manual says.

You control stitch length in free-machine quilting by moving the fabric for each stitch. Practice until you can advance the fabric evenly, making stitches about the same size. You'll probably need several hours' practice before starting a project if this procedure is new to you.

Finally . . .

You can read up on the basics of successful machine quilting, but only practice develops the right touch. These designs are just a basis for your own creative input. I hope they keep you quilting continuously.

Figure 4. Roll large projects, like the medallion center of this quilt, on either side of the needle. Safety-pin basting is done between design lines so pins stay out of stitching paths.

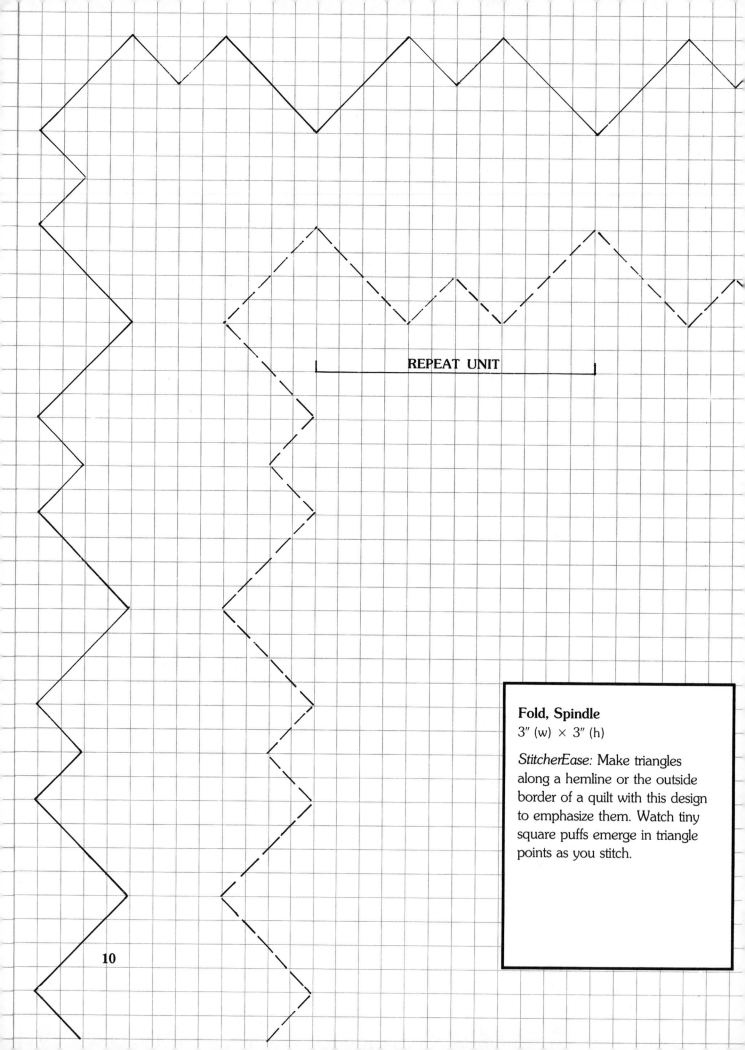

REPEAT UNIT

Fold, Spindle
3″ (w) × 3″ (h)

StitcherEase: Make triangles along a hemline or the outside border of a quilt with this design to emphasize them. Watch tiny square puffs emerge in triangle points as you stitch.

10

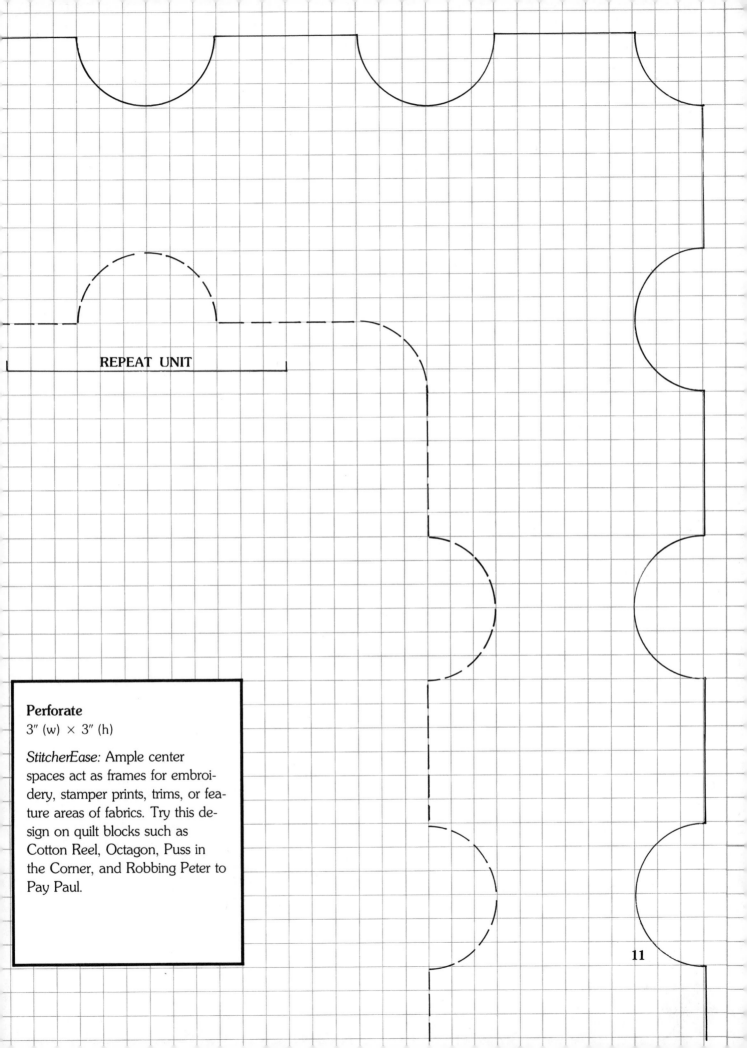

REPEAT UNIT

Perforate
3″ (w) × 3″ (h)

StitcherEase: Ample center spaces act as frames for embroidery, stamper prints, trims, or feature areas of fabrics. Try this design on quilt blocks such as Cotton Reel, Octagon, Puss in the Corner, and Robbing Peter to Pay Paul.

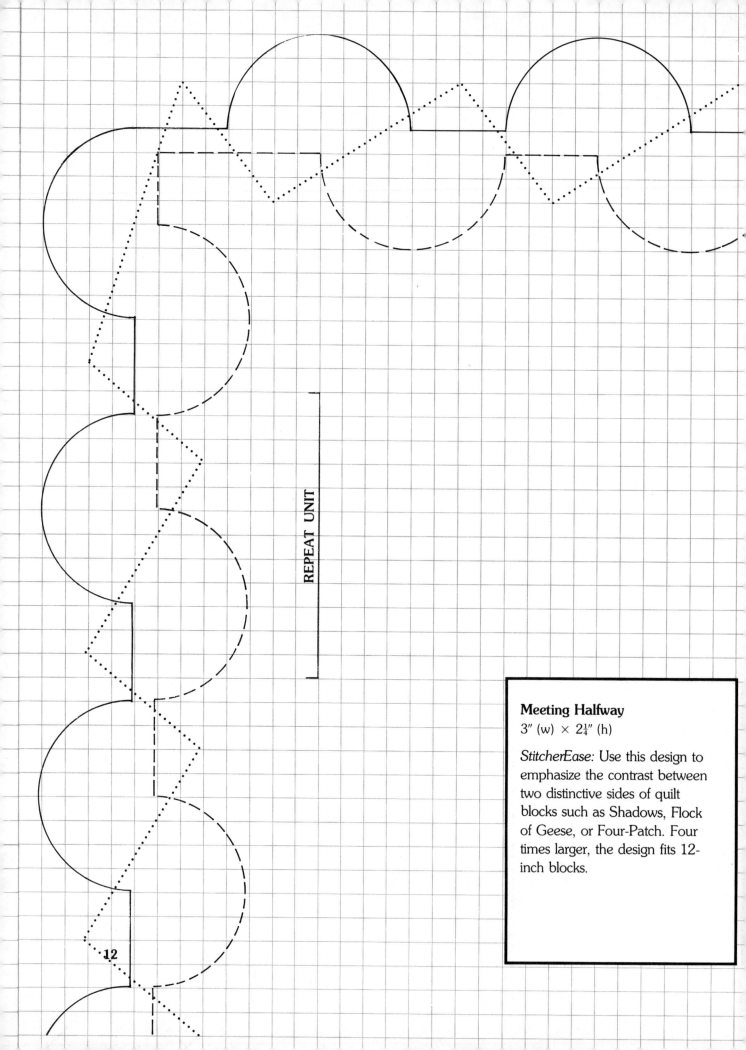

REPEAT UNIT

Meeting Halfway

3″ (w) × 2¼″ (h)

StitcherEase: Use this design to emphasize the contrast between two distinctive sides of quilt blocks such as Shadows, Flock of Geese, or Four-Patch. Four times larger, the design fits 12-inch blocks.

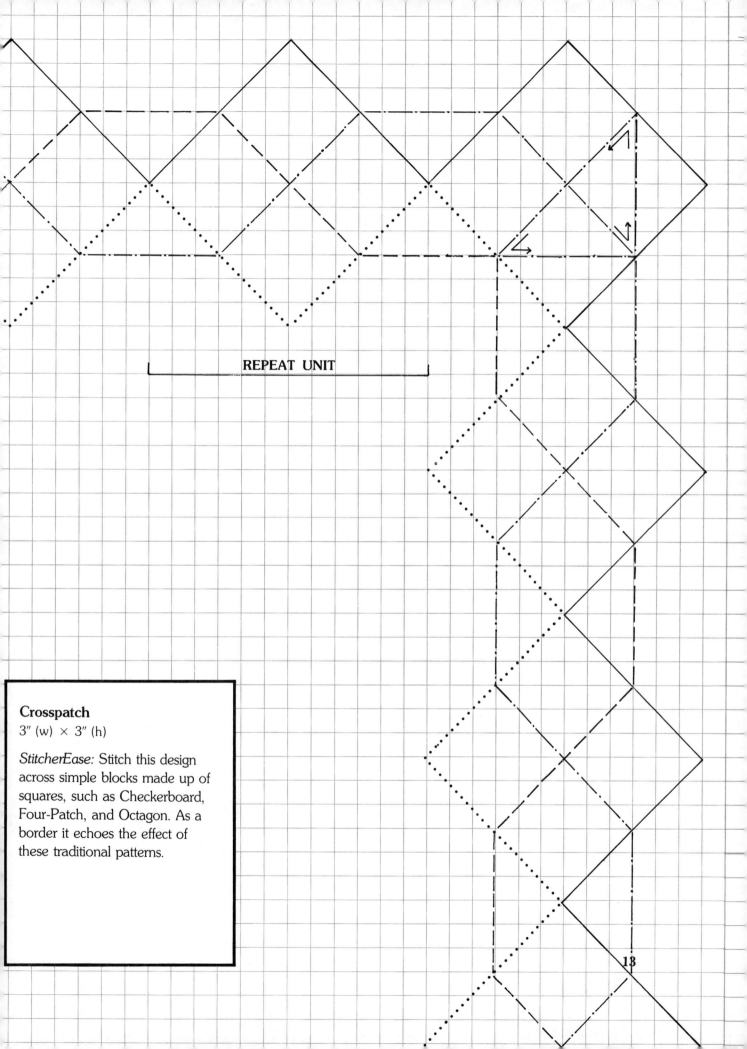

REPEAT UNIT

Crosspatch
3″ (w) × 3″ (h)

StitcherEase: Stitch this design
across simple blocks made up of
squares, such as Checkerboard,
Four-Patch, and Octagon. As a
border it echoes the effect of
these traditional patterns.

13

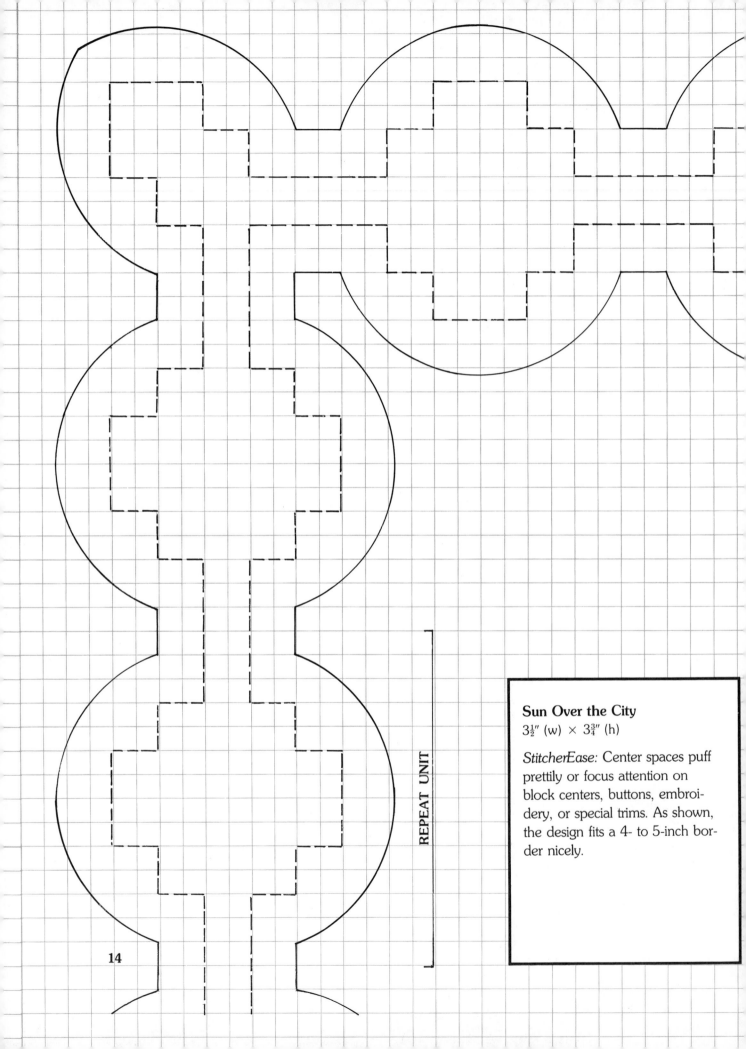

Sun Over the City
$3\frac{1}{2}''$ (w) $\times$ $3\frac{3}{4}''$ (h)

StitcherEase: Center spaces puff prettily or focus attention on block centers, buttons, embroidery, or special trims. As shown, the design fits a 4- to 5-inch border nicely.

REPEAT UNIT

14

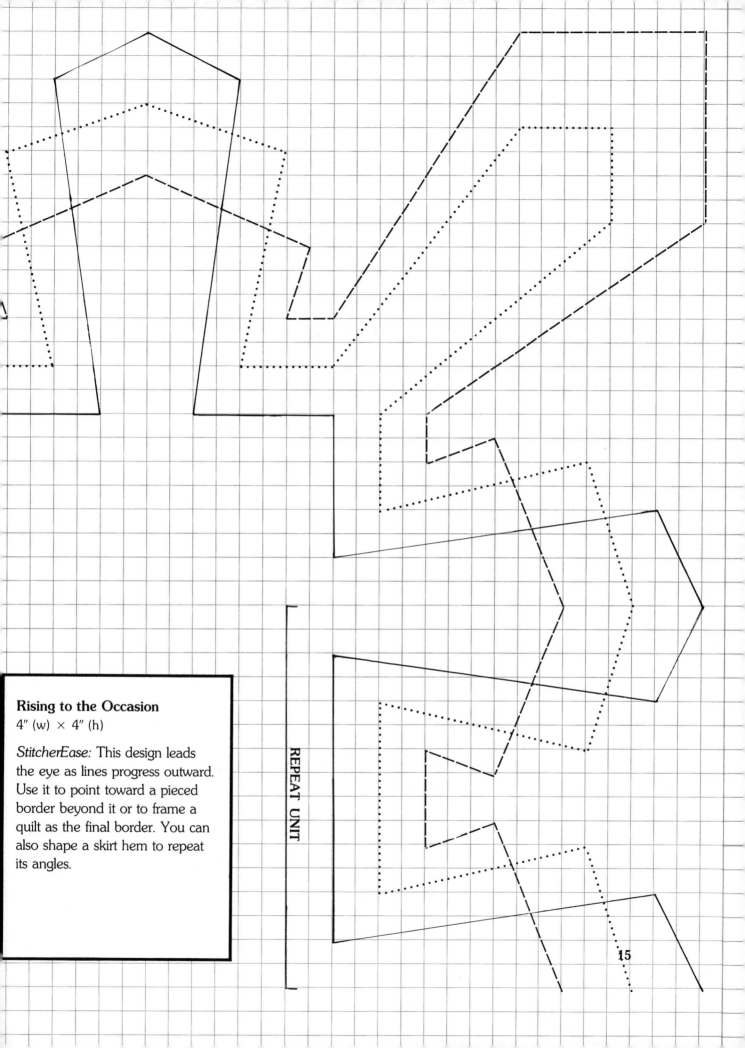

Rising to the Occasion
4″ (w) × 4″ (h)

StitcherEase: This design leads
the eye as lines progress outward.
Use it to point toward a pieced
border beyond it or to frame a
quilt as the final border. You can
also shape a skirt hem to repeat
its angles.

REPEAT UNIT

15

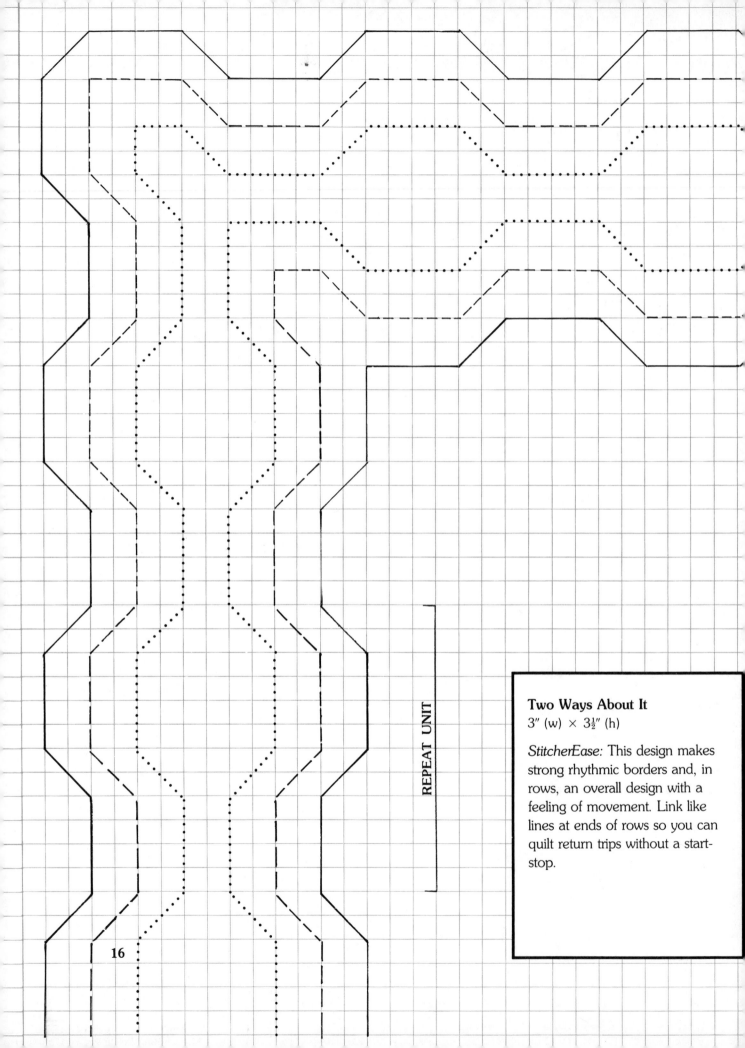

REPEAT UNIT

Two Ways About It
3″ (w) × 3½″ (h)

StitcherEase: This design makes strong rhythmic borders and, in rows, an overall design with a feeling of movement. Link like lines at ends of rows so you can quilt return trips without a start-stop.

16

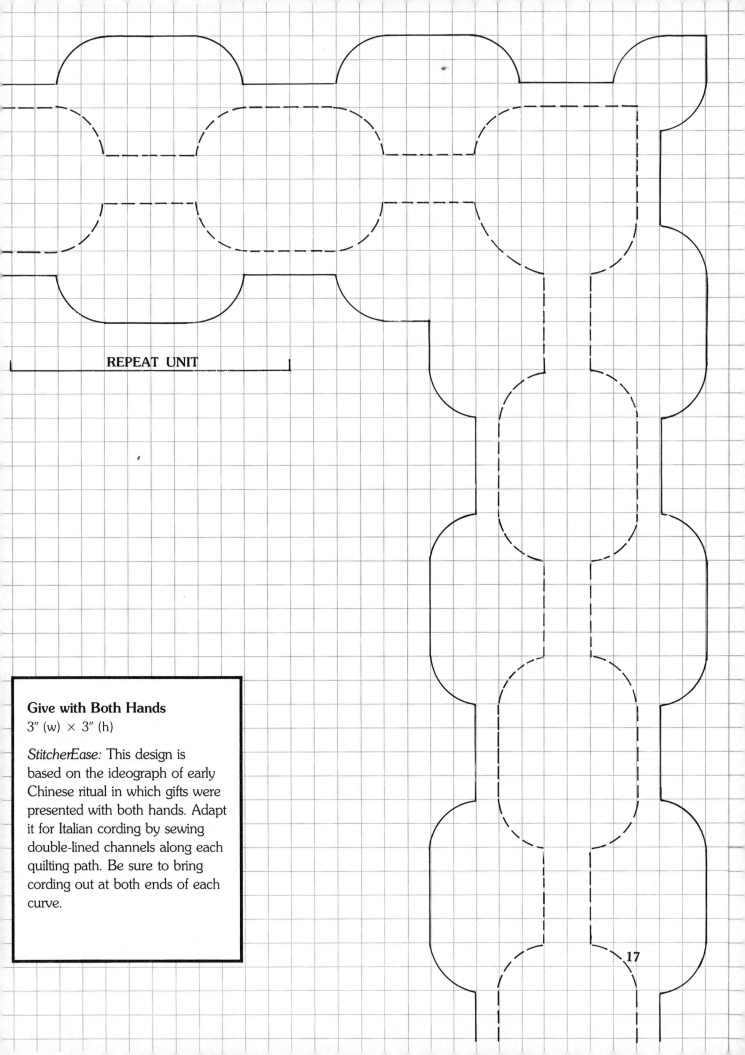

REPEAT UNIT

Give with Both Hands
3″ (w) × 3″ (h)

StitcherEase: This design is based on the ideograph of early Chinese ritual in which gifts were presented with both hands. Adapt it for Italian cording by sewing double-lined channels along each quilting path. Be sure to bring cording out at both ends of each curve.

17

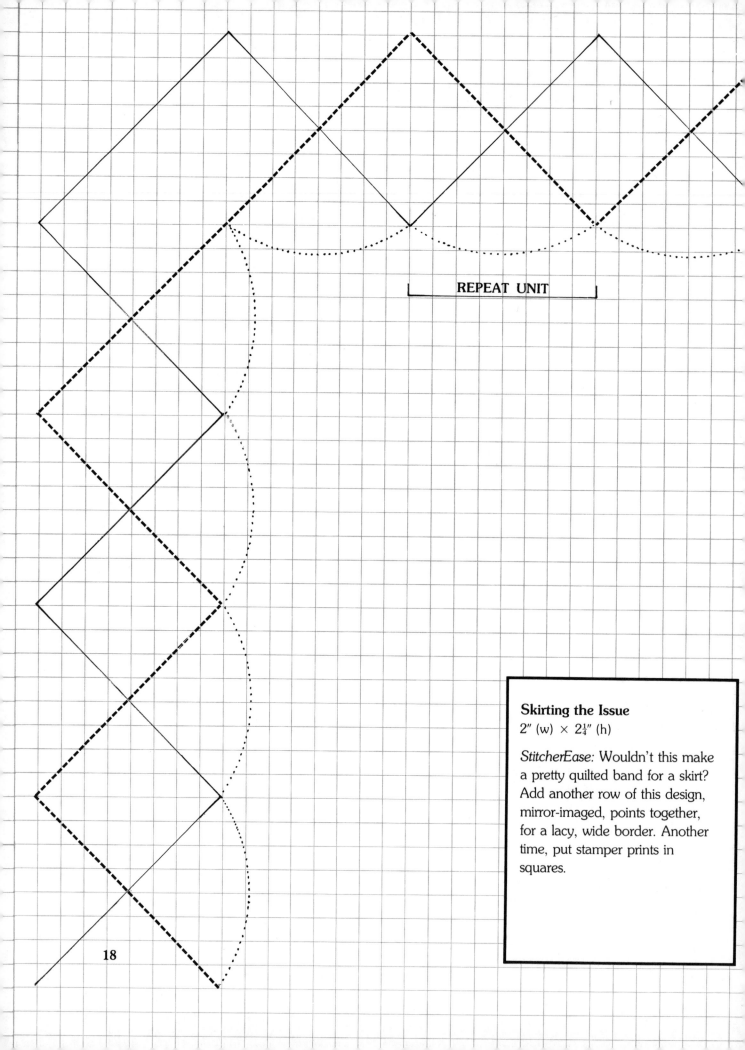

REPEAT UNIT

Skirting the Issue
2″ (w) × 2¼″ (h)

StitcherEase: Wouldn't this make a pretty quilted band for a skirt? Add another row of this design, mirror-imaged, points together, for a lacy, wide border. Another time, put stamper prints in squares.

18

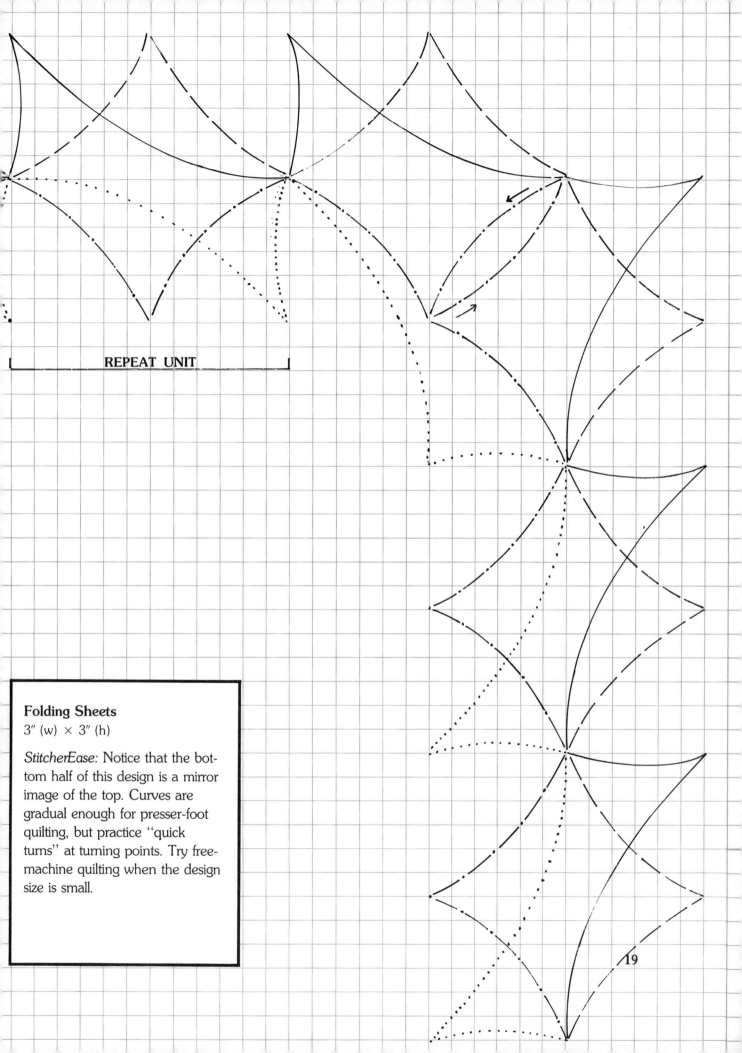

REPEAT UNIT

Folding Sheets
3″ (w) × 3″ (h)

StitcherEase: Notice that the bottom half of this design is a mirror image of the top. Curves are gradual enough for presser-foot quilting, but practice "quick turns" at turning points. Try free-machine quilting when the design size is small.

19

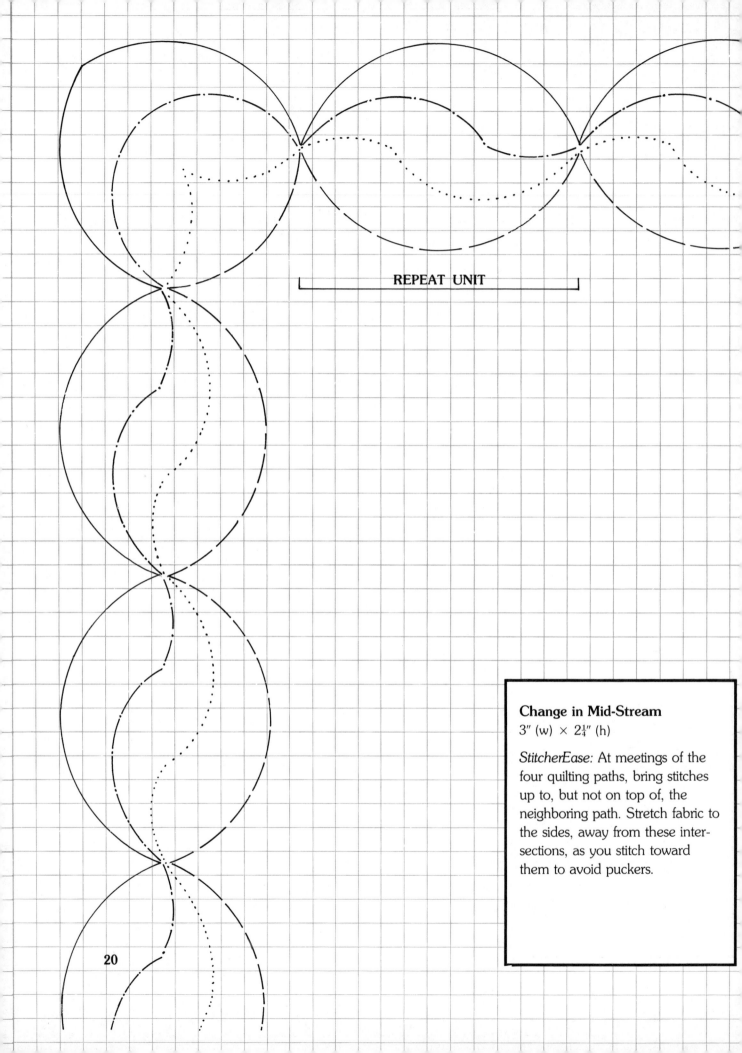

REPEAT UNIT

Change in Mid-Stream
3″ (w) × 2¼″ (h)

StitcherEase: At meetings of the four quilting paths, bring stitches up to, but not on top of, the neighboring path. Stretch fabric to the sides, away from these inter-sections, as you stitch toward them to avoid puckers.

20

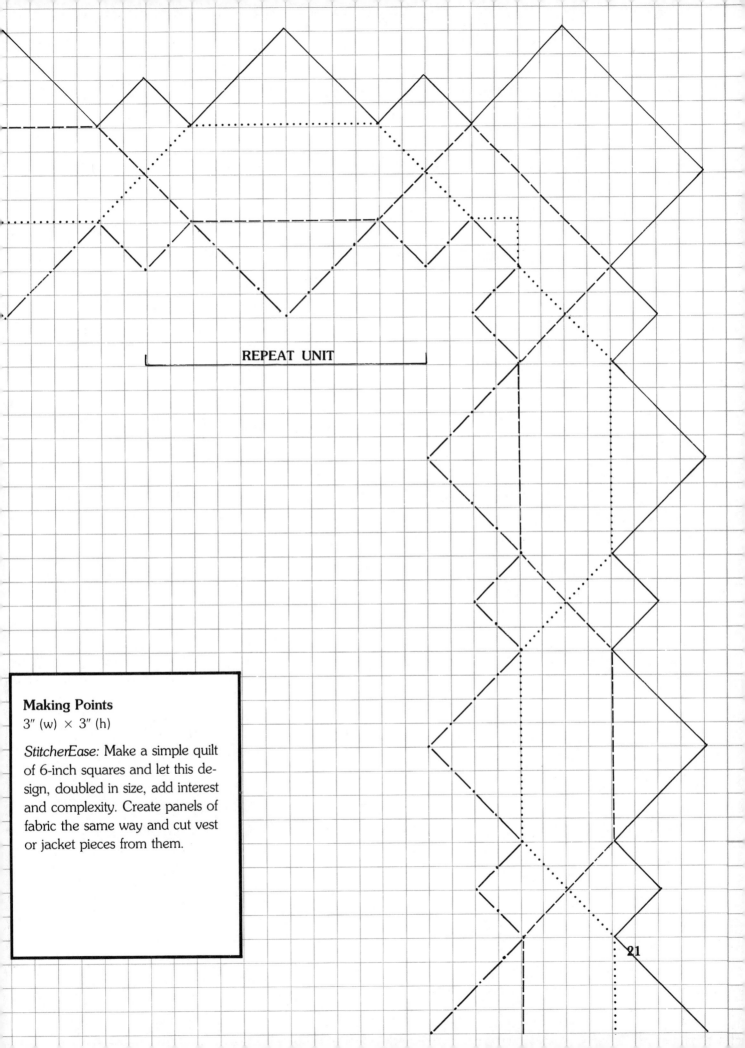

REPEAT UNIT

Making Points
3″ (w) × 3″ (h)

StitcherEase: Make a simple quilt of 6-inch squares and let this design, doubled in size, add interest and complexity. Create panels of fabric the same way and cut vest or jacket pieces from them.

21

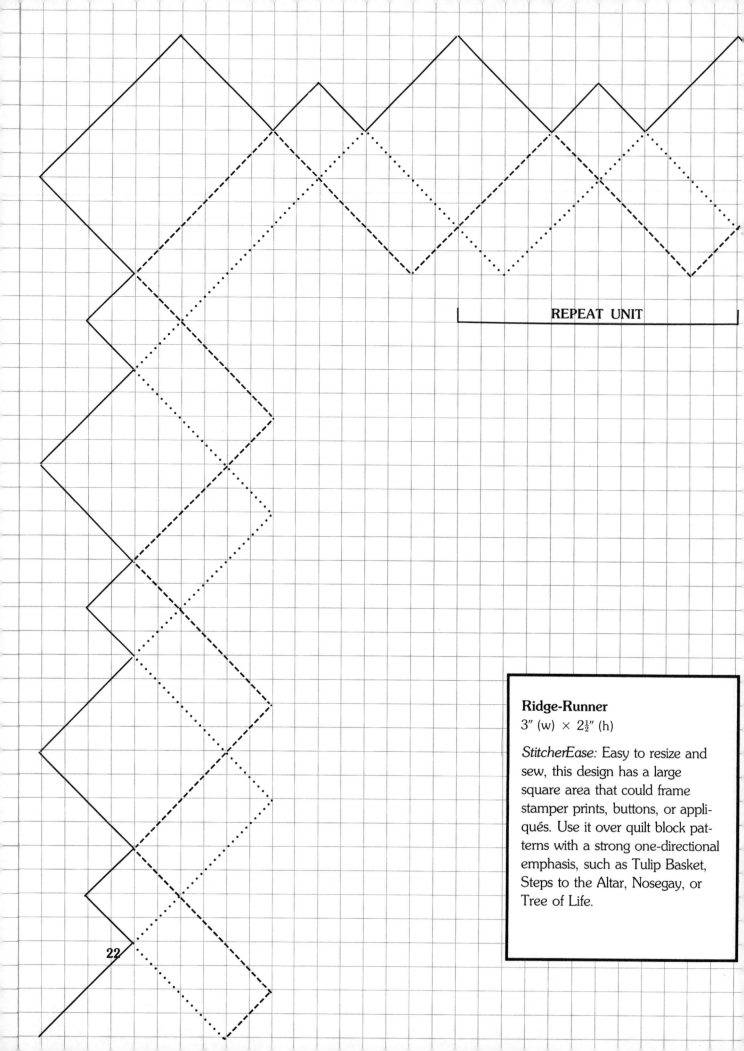

REPEAT UNIT

Ridge-Runner
3″ (w) × 2½″ (h)

StitcherEase: Easy to resize and
sew, this design has a large
square area that could frame
stamper prints, buttons, or appliqués. Use it over quilt block patterns with a strong one-directional
emphasis, such as Tulip Basket,
Steps to the Altar, Nosegay, or
Tree of Life.

22

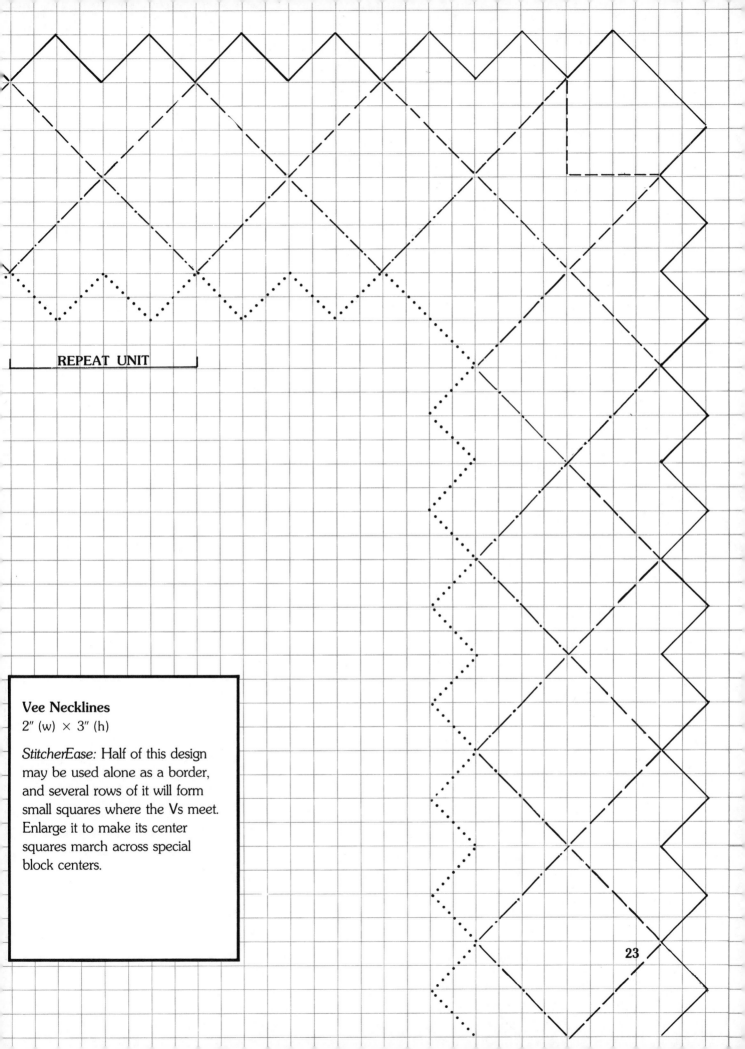

REPEAT UNIT

Vee Necklines
2″ (w) × 3″ (h)

StitcherEase: Half of this design
may be used alone as a border,
and several rows of it will form
small squares where the Vs meet.
Enlarge it to make its center
squares march across special
block centers.

23

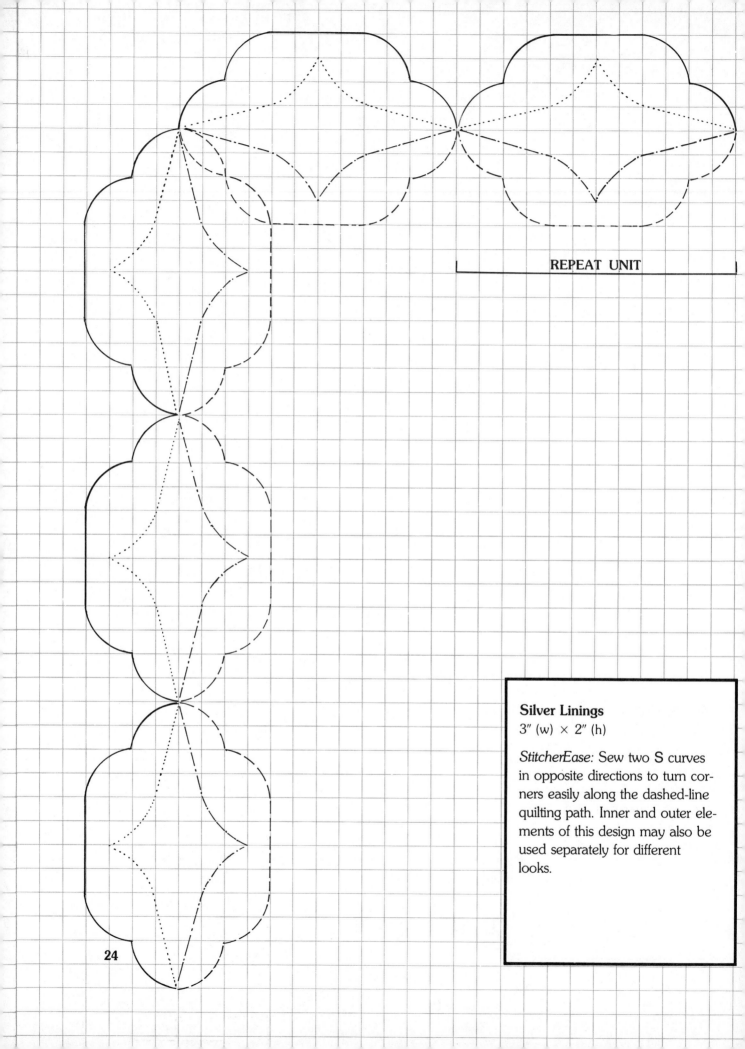

REPEAT UNIT

Silver Linings
3″ (w) × 2″ (h)

StitcherEase: Sew two **S** curves in opposite directions to turn corners easily along the dashed-line quilting path. Inner and outer elements of this design may also be used separately for different looks.

24

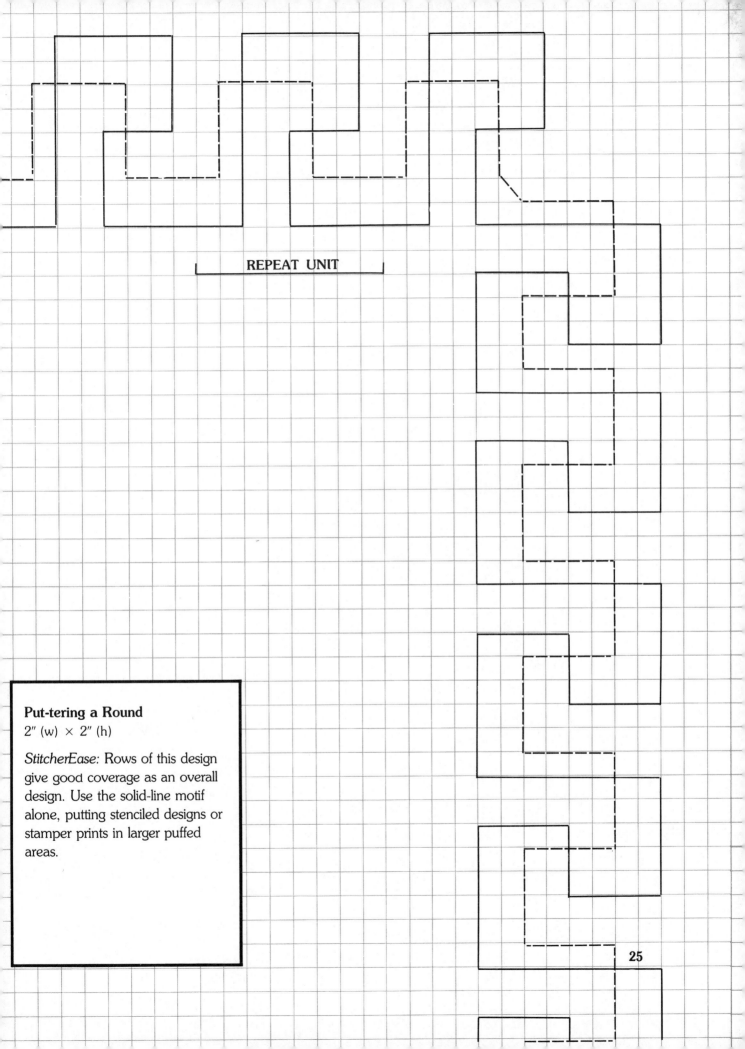

REPEAT UNIT

Put-tering a Round
2″ (w) × 2″ (h)

StitcherEase: Rows of this design give good coverage as an overall design. Use the solid-line motif alone, putting stenciled designs or stamper prints in larger puffed areas.

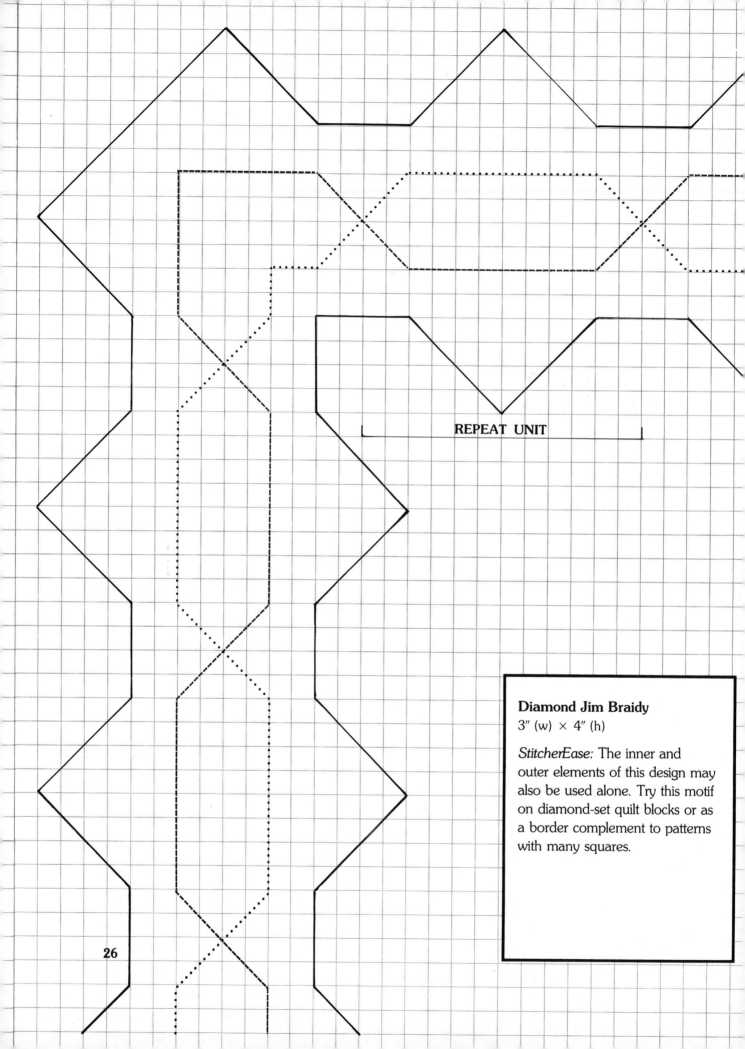

REPEAT UNIT

Diamond Jim Braidy
3″ (w) × 4″ (h)

StitcherEase: The inner and outer elements of this design may also be used alone. Try this motif on diamond-set quilt blocks or as a border complement to patterns with many squares.

26

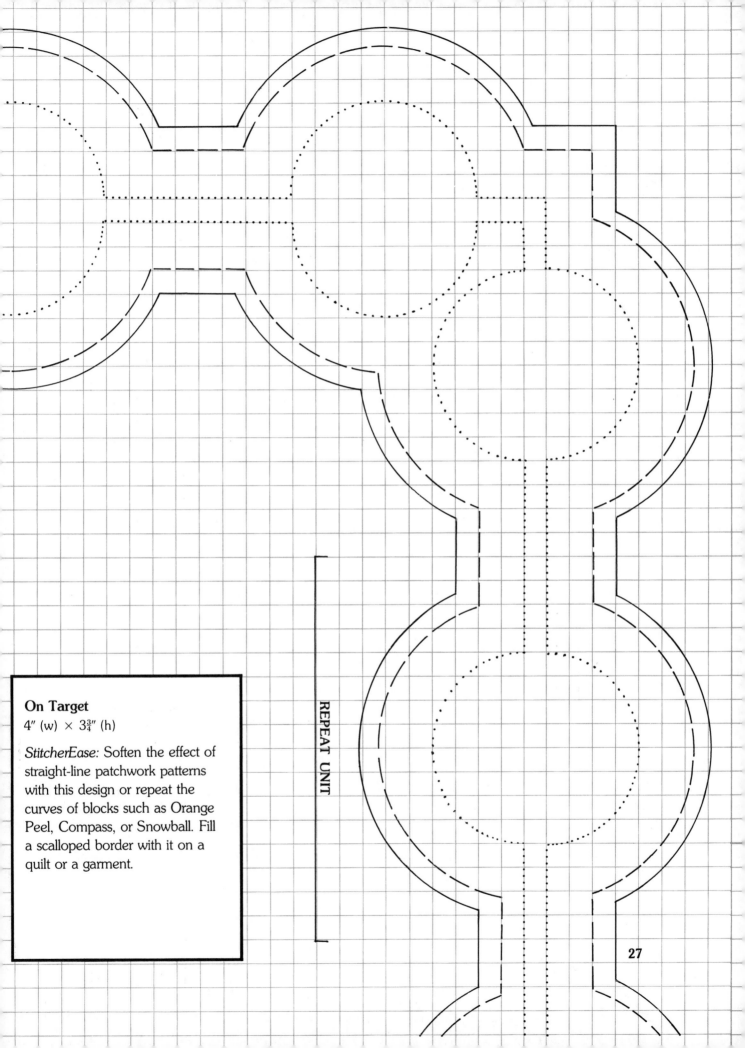

On Target

4″ (w) × 3¾″ (h)

StitcherEase: Soften the effect of straight-line patchwork patterns with this design or repeat the curves of blocks such as Orange Peel, Compass, or Snowball. Fill a scalloped border with it on a quilt or a garment.

REPEAT UNIT

27

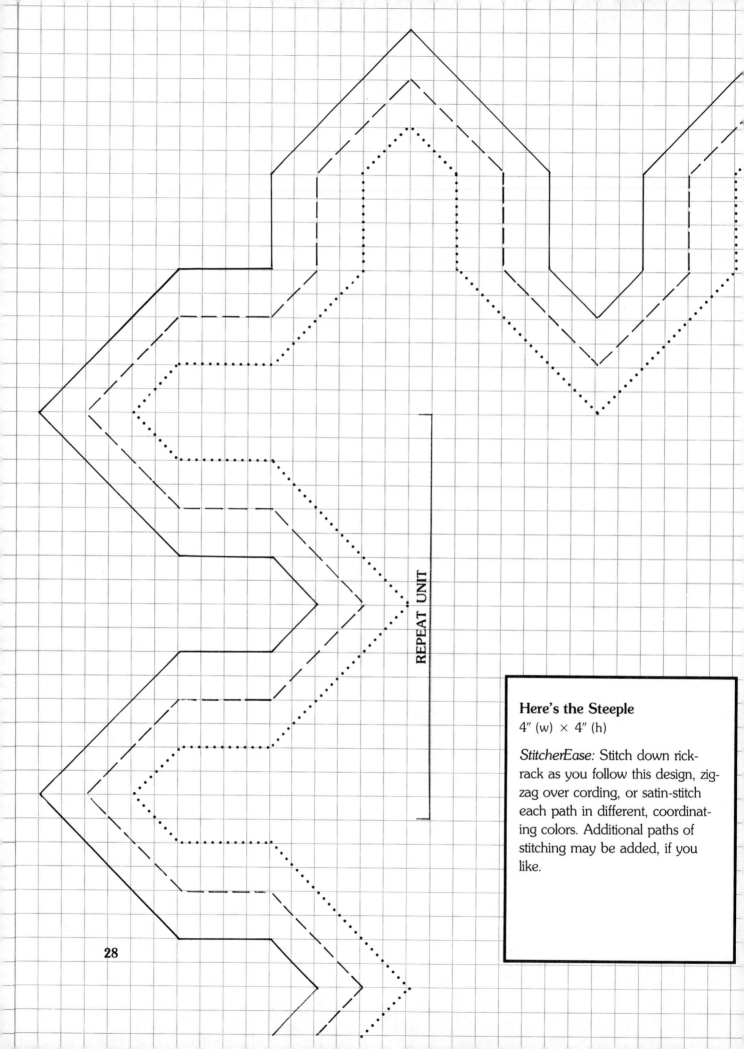

REPEAT UNIT

Here's the Steeple
4″ (w) × 4″ (h)

StitcherEase: Stitch down rick-rack as you follow this design, zig-zag over cording, or satin-stitch each path in different, coordinating colors. Additional paths of stitching may be added, if you like.

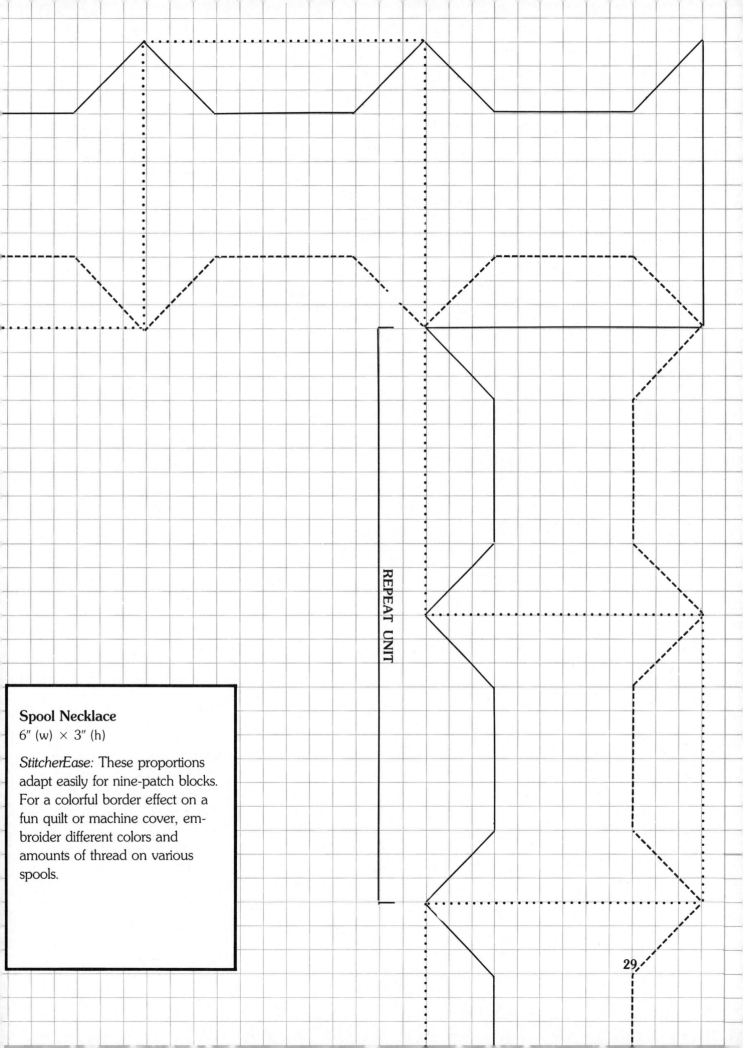

REPEAT UNIT

Spool Necklace

6″ (w) × 3″ (h)

StitcherEase: These proportions adapt easily for nine-patch blocks. For a colorful border effect on a fun quilt or machine cover, embroider different colors and amounts of thread on various spools.

29

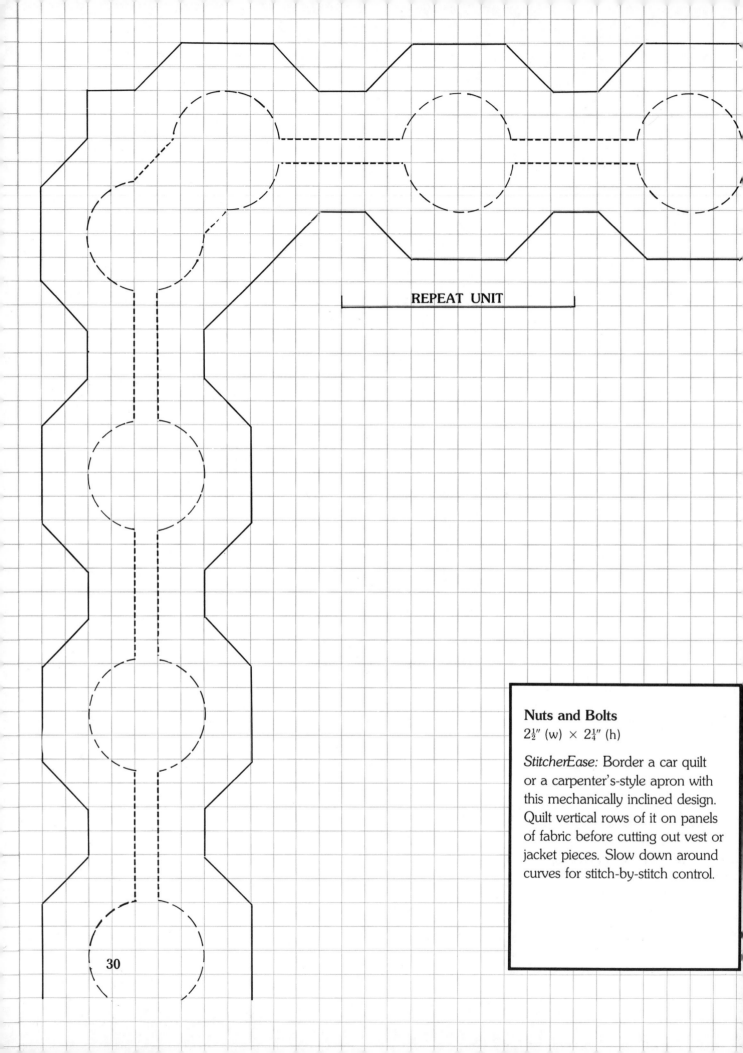

REPEAT UNIT

Nuts and Bolts
$2\frac{1}{2}''$ (w) × $2\frac{1}{4}''$ (h)

StitcherEase: Border a car quilt or a carpenter's-style apron with this mechanically inclined design. Quilt vertical rows of it on panels of fabric before cutting out vest or jacket pieces. Slow down around curves for stitch-by-stitch control.

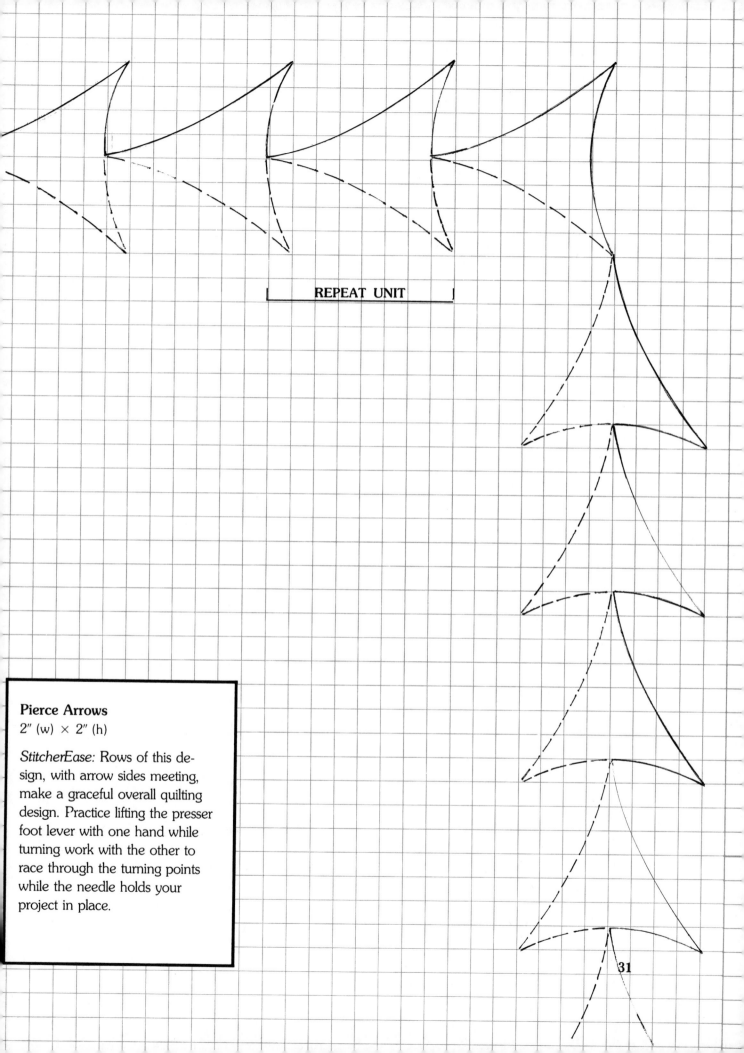

REPEAT UNIT

Pierce Arrows

2″ (w) × 2″ (h)

StitcherEase: Rows of this design, with arrow sides meeting, make a graceful overall quilting design. Practice lifting the presser foot lever with one hand while turning work with the other to race through the turning points while the needle holds your project in place.

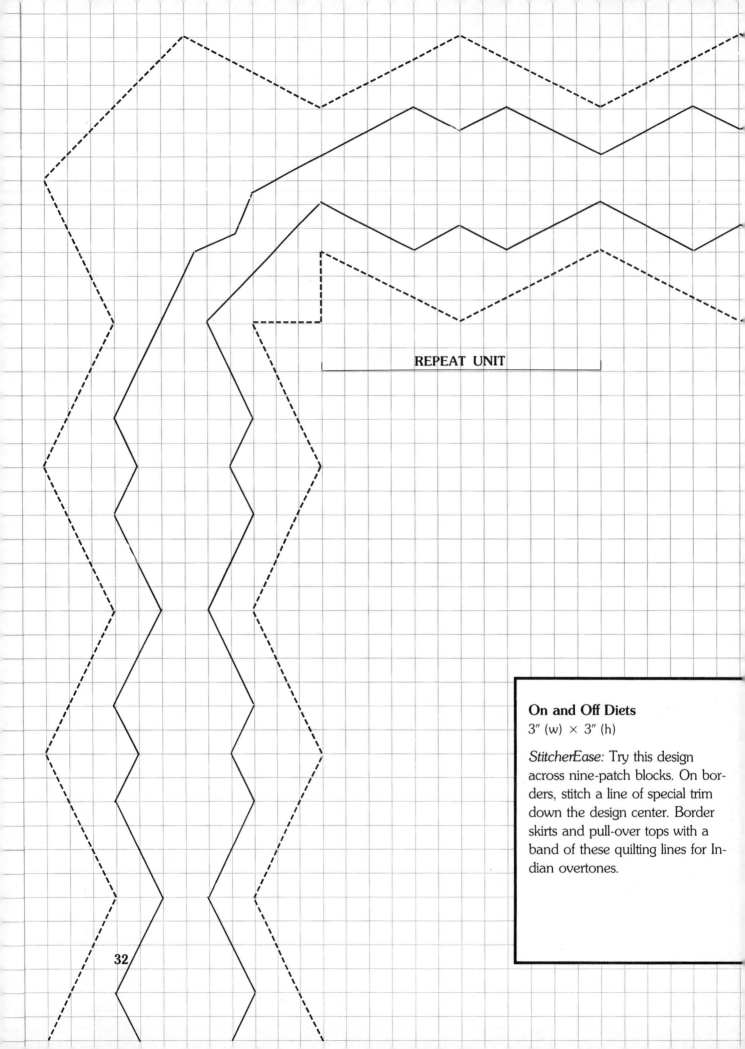

REPEAT UNIT

On and Off Diets
3″ (w) × 3″ (h)

StitcherEase: Try this design across nine-patch blocks. On borders, stitch a line of special trim down the design center. Border skirts and pull-over tops with a band of these quilting lines for Indian overtones.

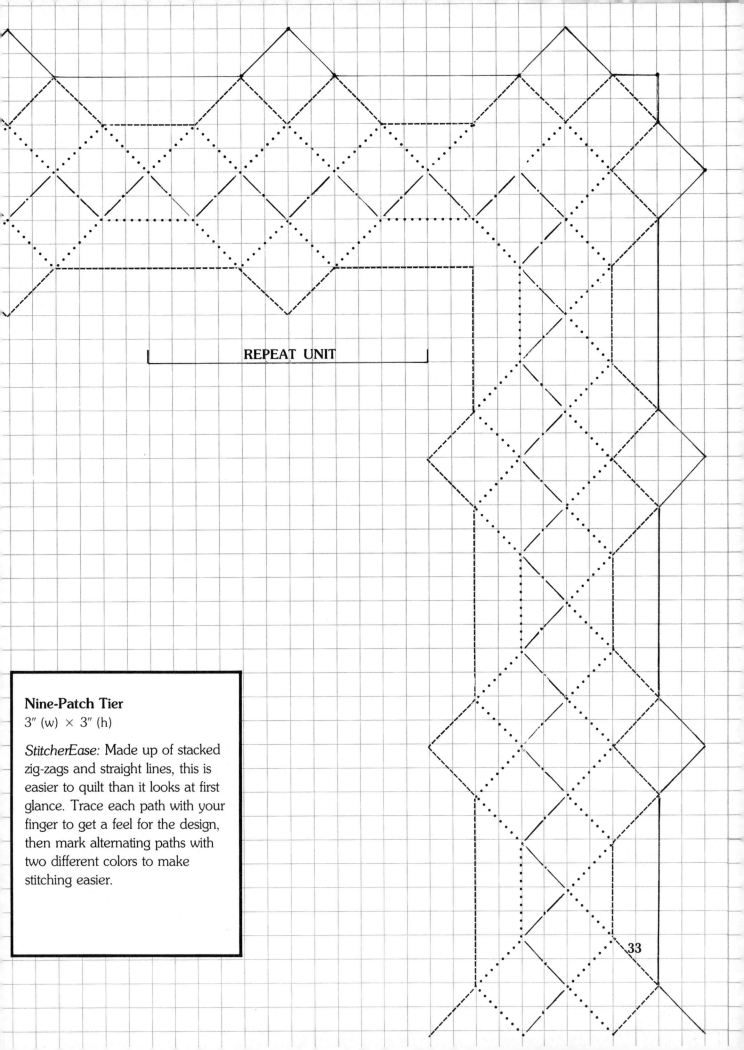

REPEAT UNIT

Nine-Patch Tier
3″ (w) × 3″ (h)

StitcherEase: Made up of stacked zig-zags and straight lines, this is easier to quilt than it looks at first glance. Trace each path with your finger to get a feel for the design, then mark alternating paths with two different colors to make stitching easier.

33

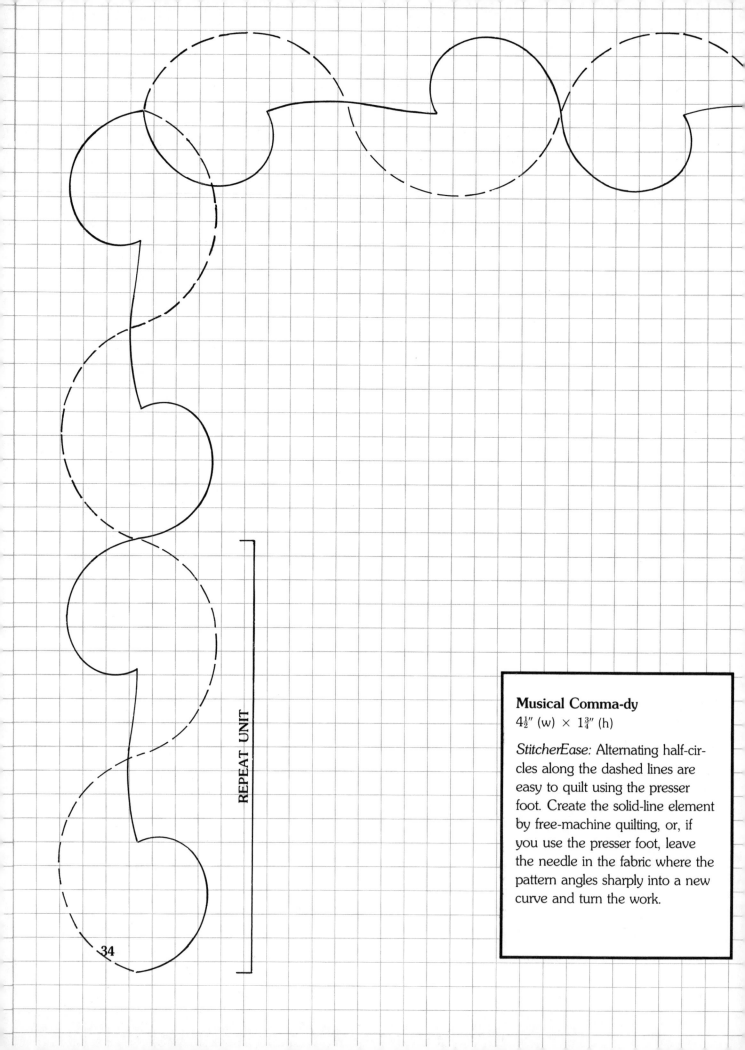

REPEAT UNIT

Musical Comma-dy
$4\frac{1}{2}''$ (w) $\times$ $1\frac{3}{4}''$ (h)

StitcherEase: Alternating half-circles along the dashed lines are easy to quilt using the presser foot. Create the solid-line element by free-machine quilting, or, if you use the presser foot, leave the needle in the fabric where the pattern angles sharply into a new curve and turn the work.

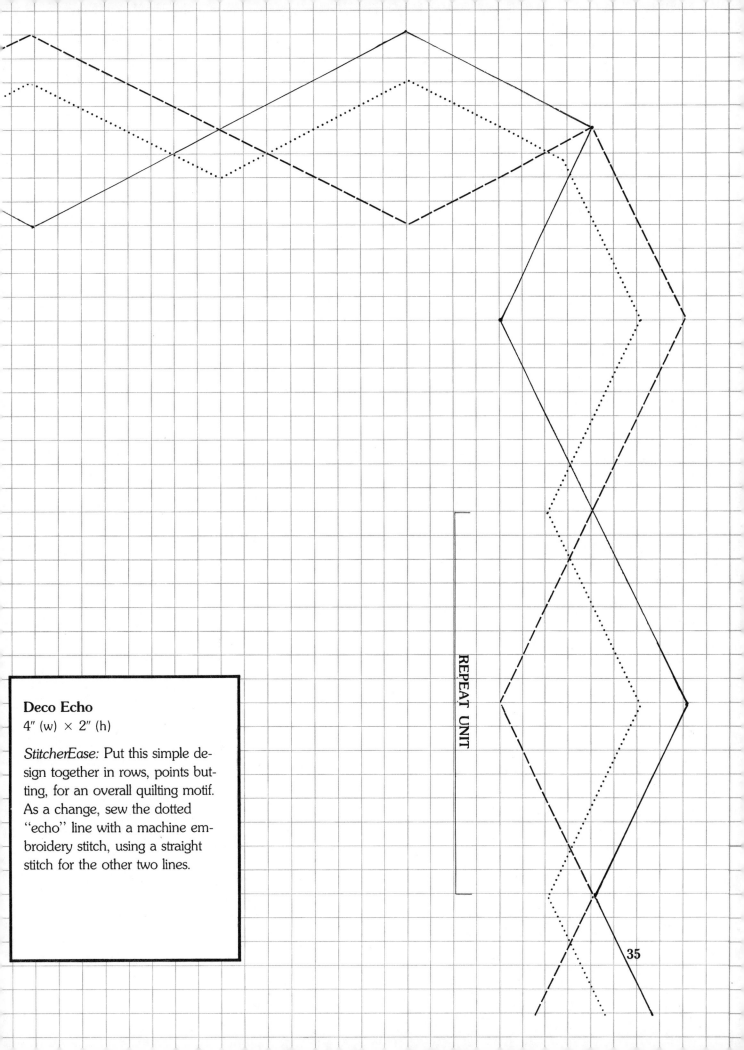

Deco Echo
4″ (w) × 2″ (h)

StitcherEase: Put this simple design together in rows, points butting, for an overall quilting motif. As a change, sew the dotted "echo" line with a machine embroidery stitch, using a straight stitch for the other two lines.

REPEAT UNIT

35

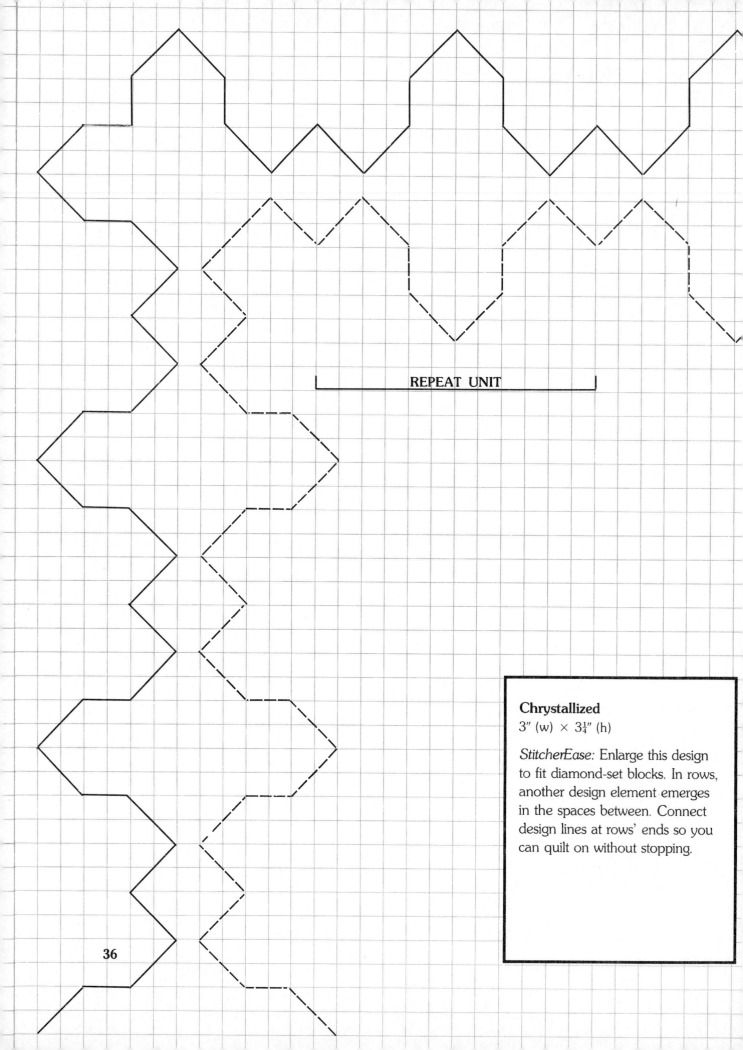

REPEAT UNIT

Chrystallized
3″ (w) × 3¼″ (h)

StitcherEase: Enlarge this design
to fit diamond-set blocks. In rows,
another design element emerges
in the spaces between. Connect
design lines at rows' ends so you
can quilt on without stopping.

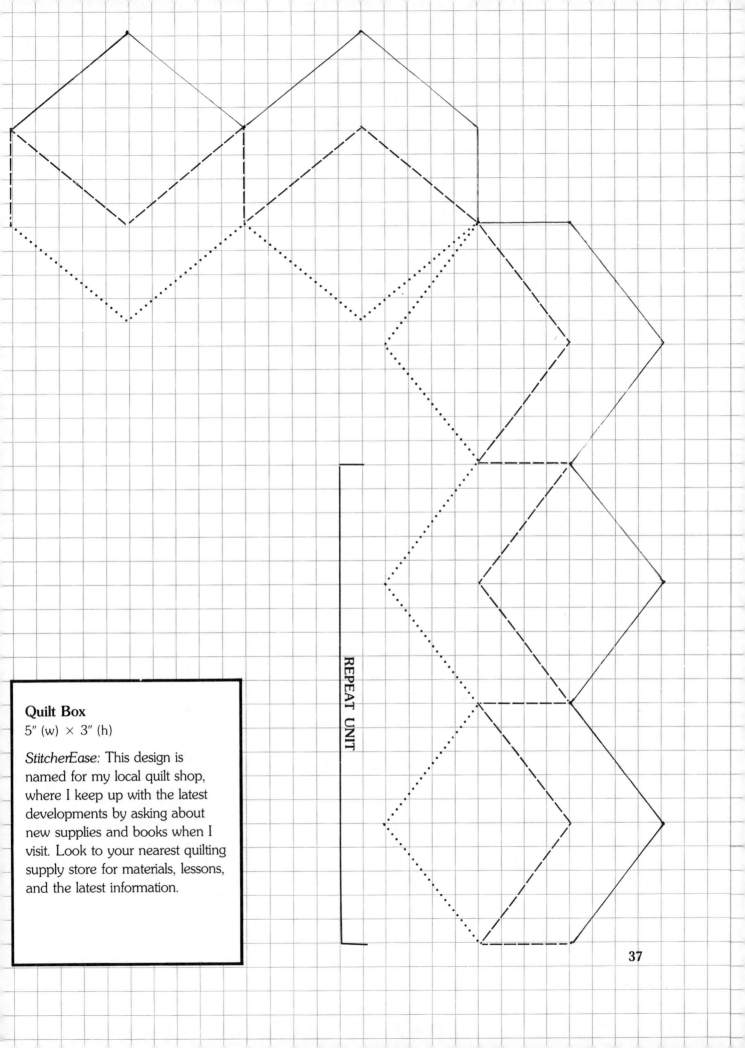

Quilt Box

5″ (w) × 3″ (h)

StitcherEase: This design is named for my local quilt shop, where I keep up with the latest developments by asking about new supplies and books when I visit. Look to your nearest quilting supply store for materials, lessons, and the latest information.

REPEAT UNIT

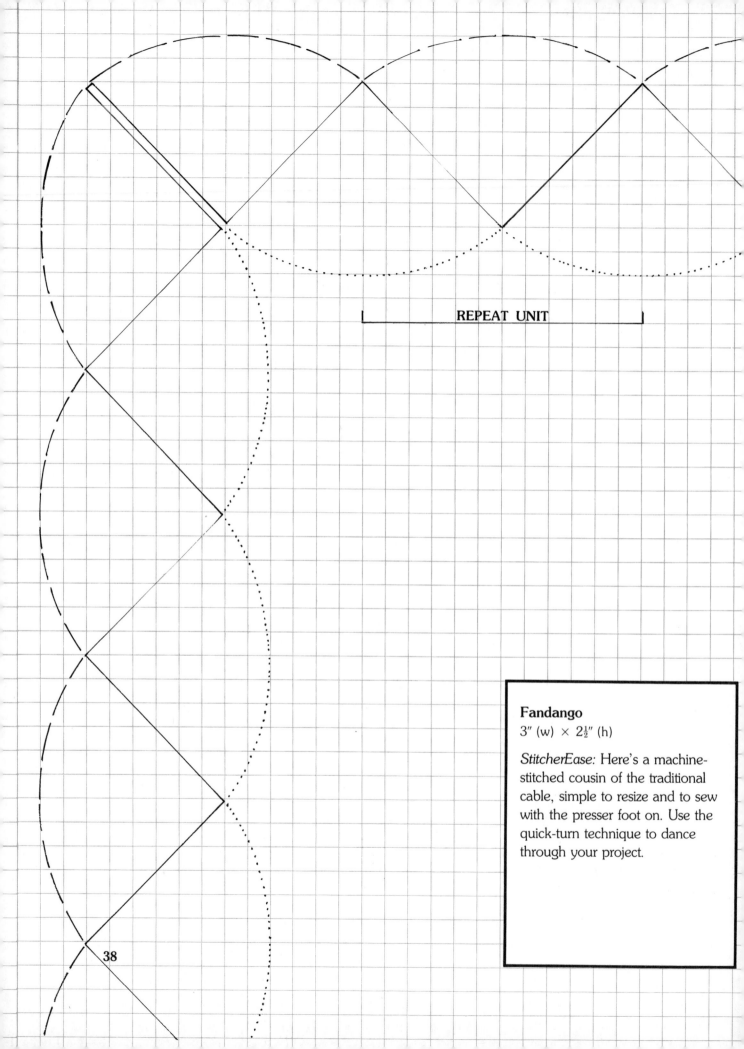

REPEAT UNIT

Fandango
3″ (w) × 2½″ (h)

StitcherEase: Here's a machine-stitched cousin of the traditional cable, simple to resize and to sew with the presser foot on. Use the quick-turn technique to dance through your project.

38

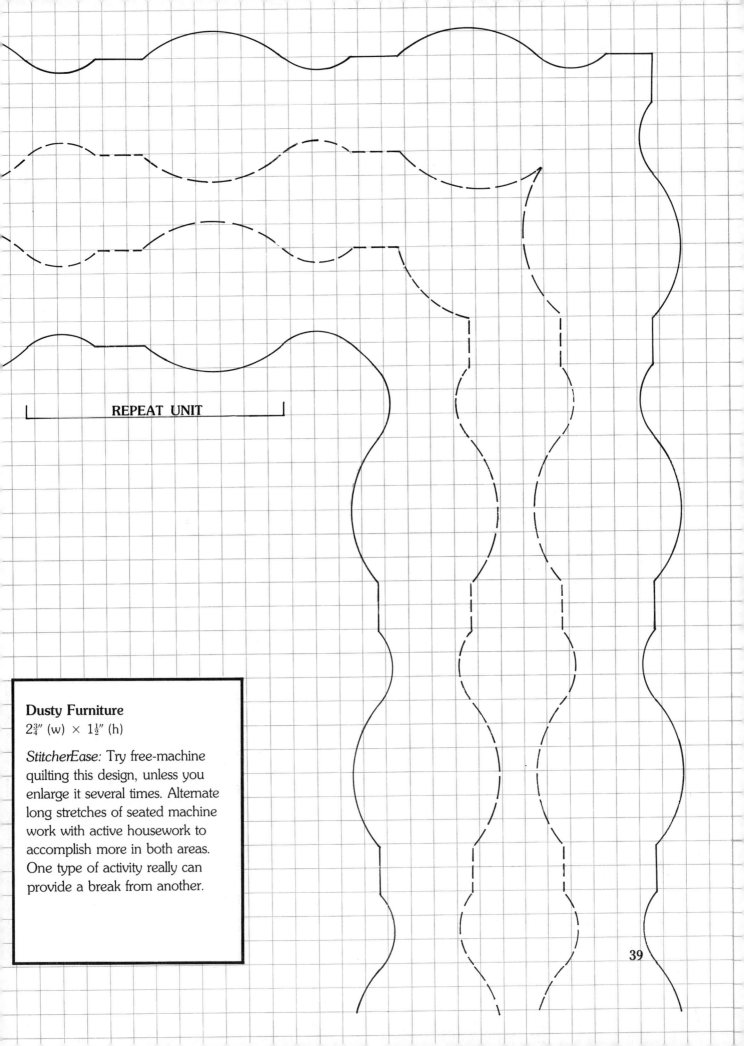

REPEAT UNIT

Dusty Furniture
$2\frac{3}{4}''$ (w) $\times$ $1\frac{1}{2}''$ (h)

StitcherEase: Try free-machine quilting this design, unless you enlarge it several times. Alternate long stretches of seated machine work with active housework to accomplish more in both areas. One type of activity really can provide a break from another.

39

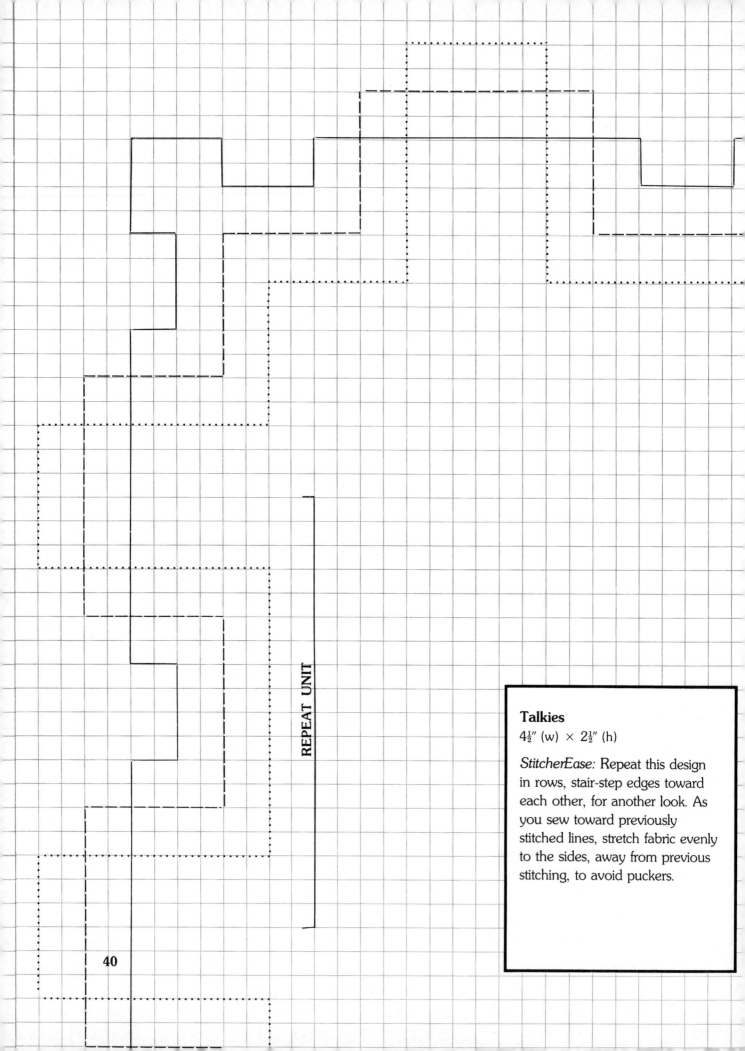

REPEAT UNIT

Talkies

$4\frac{1}{2}''$ (w) $\times$ $2\frac{1}{2}''$ (h)

StitcherEase: Repeat this design in rows, stair-step edges toward each other, for another look. As you sew toward previously stitched lines, stretch fabric evenly to the sides, away from previous stitching, to avoid puckers.

40

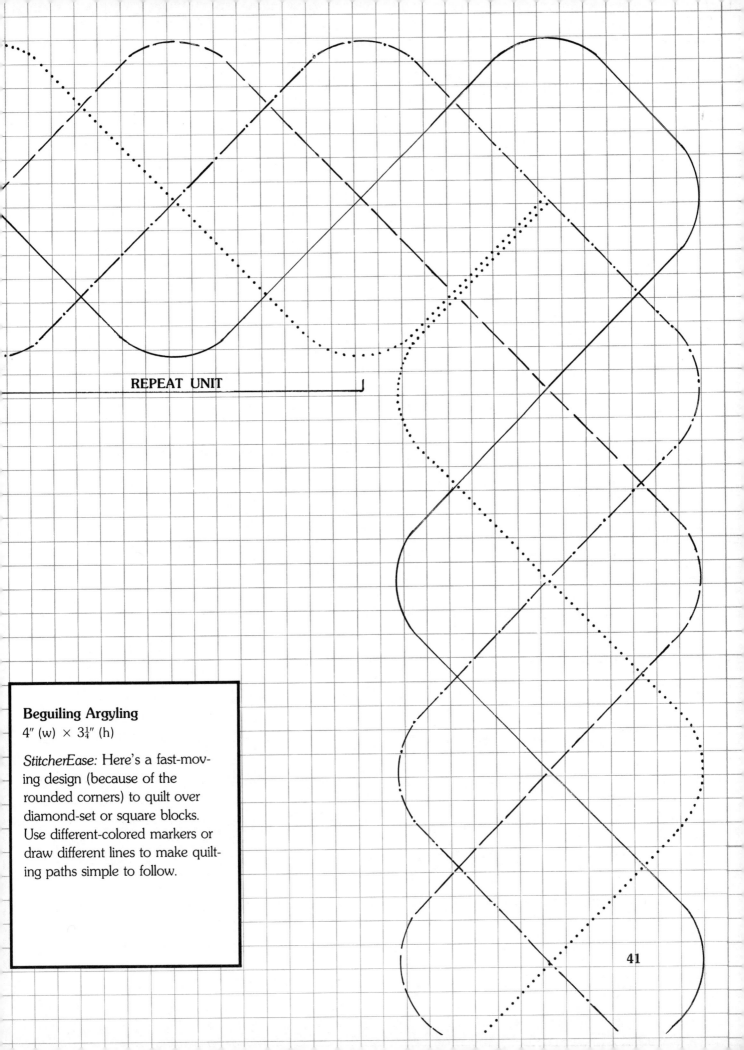

REPEAT UNIT

Beguiling Argyling
4″ (w) × 3¼″ (h)

StitcherEase: Here's a fast-moving design (because of the rounded corners) to quilt over diamond-set or square blocks. Use different-colored markers or draw different lines to make quilting paths simple to follow.

41

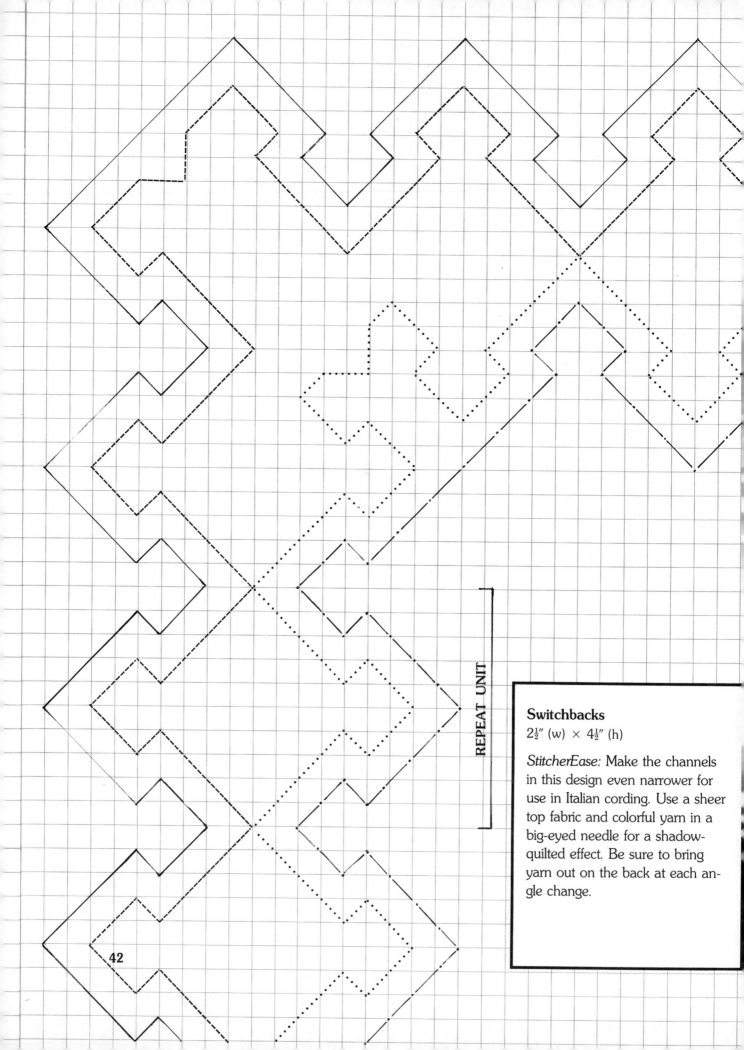

REPEAT UNIT

Switchbacks

$2\frac{1}{2}''$ (w) $\times$ $4\frac{1}{2}''$ (h)

StitcherEase: Make the channels in this design even narrower for use in Italian cording. Use a sheer top fabric and colorful yarn in a big-eyed needle for a shadow-quilted effect. Be sure to bring yarn out on the back at each angle change.

42

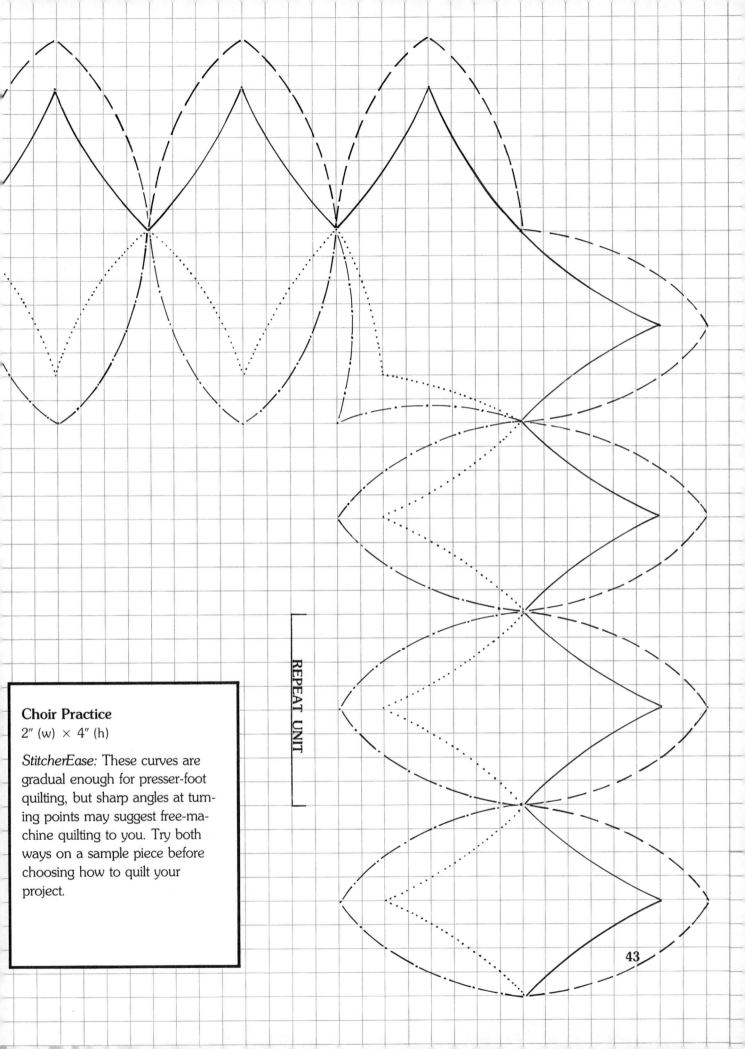

Choir Practice
2″ (w) × 4″ (h)

StitcherEase: These curves are gradual enough for presser-foot quilting, but sharp angles at turning points may suggest free-machine quilting to you. Try both ways on a sample piece before choosing how to quilt your project.

REPEAT UNIT

43

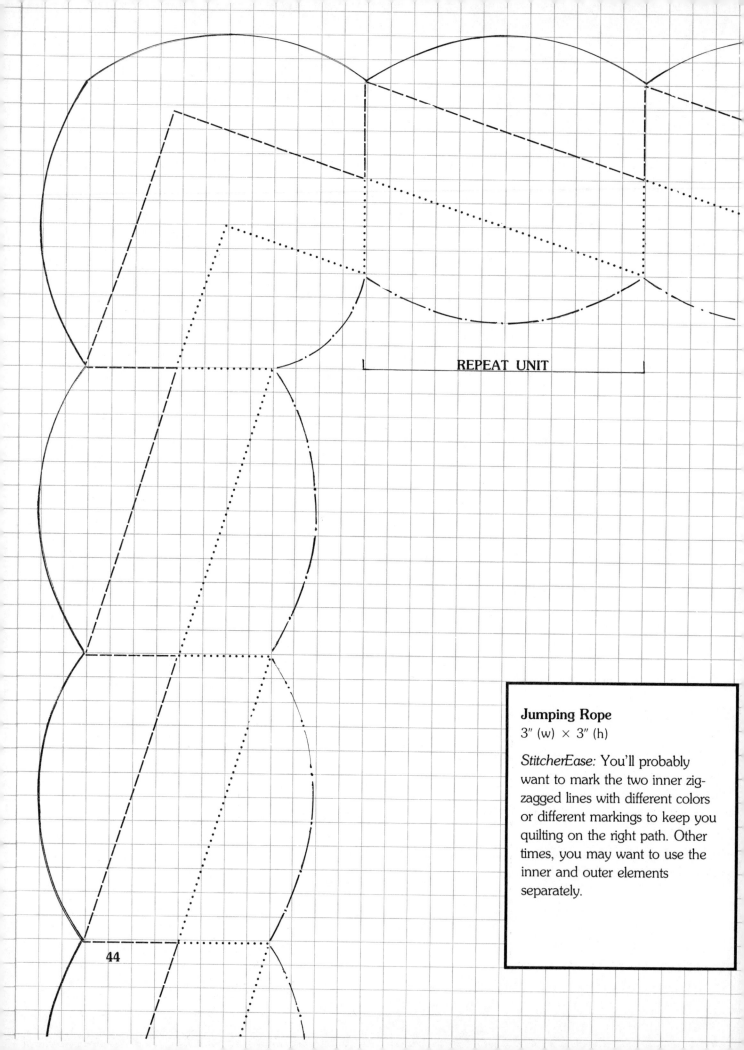

REPEAT UNIT

Jumping Rope
3″ (w) × 3″ (h)

StitcherEase: You'll probably want to mark the two inner zig-zagged lines with different colors or different markings to keep you quilting on the right path. Other times, you may want to use the inner and outer elements separately.

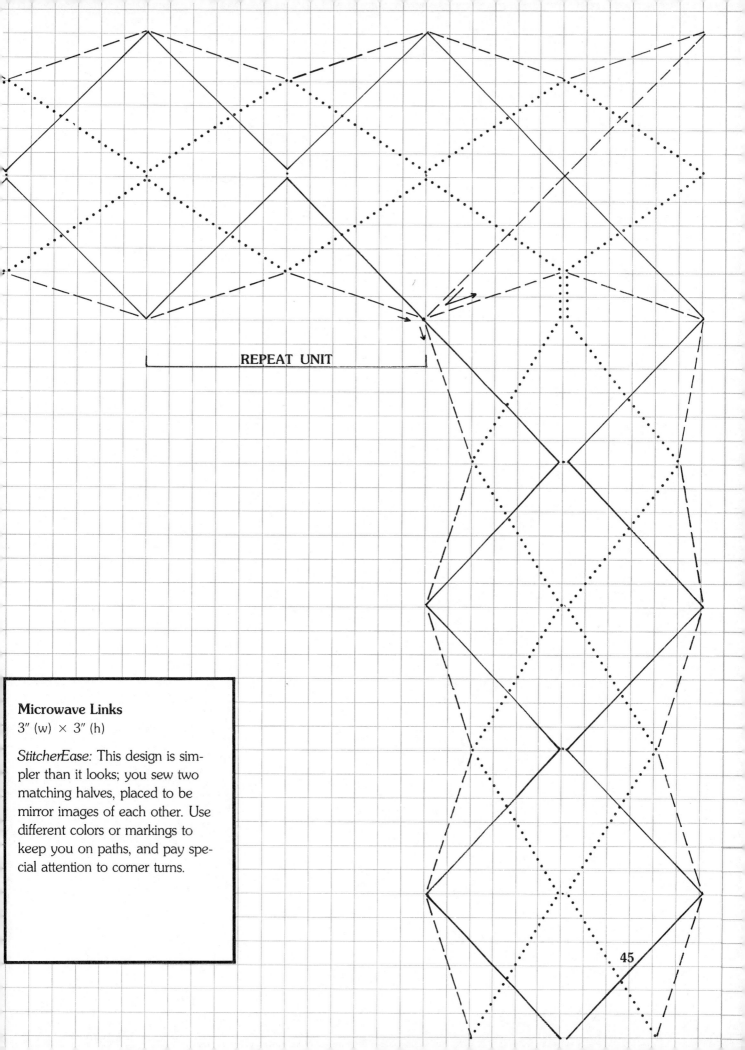

REPEAT UNIT

Microwave Links
3″ (w) × 3″ (h)

StitcherEase: This design is simpler than it looks; you sew two matching halves, placed to be mirror images of each other. Use different colors or markings to keep you on paths, and pay special attention to corner turns.

45

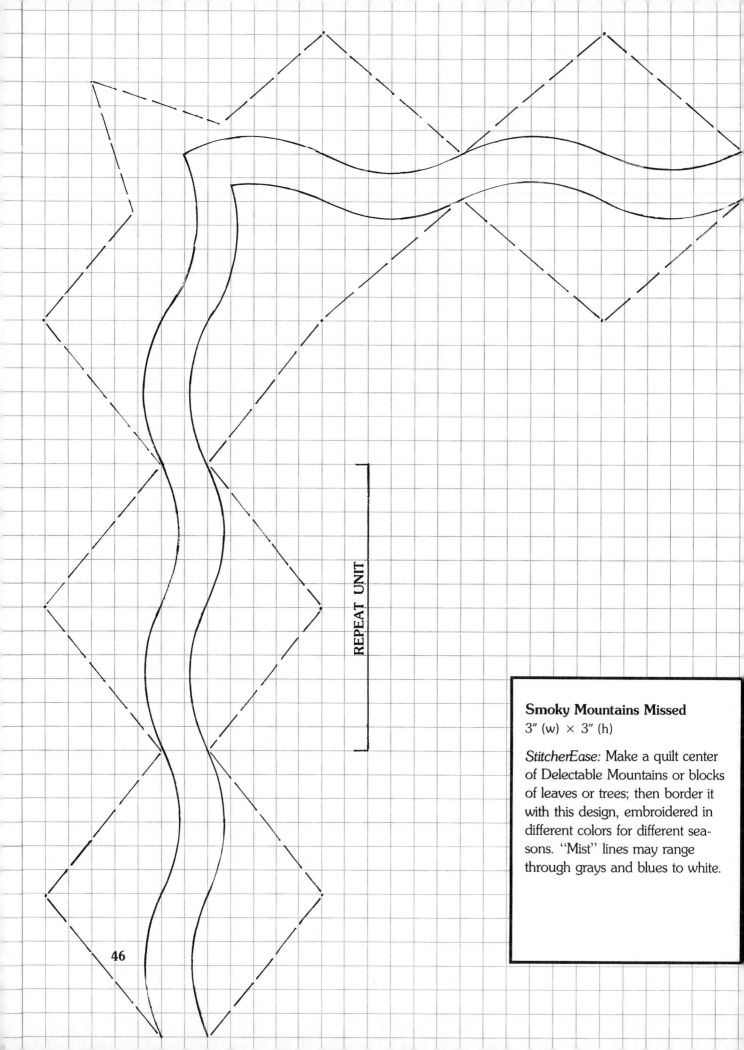

REPEAT UNIT

46

Smoky Mountains Missed
3″ (w) × 3″ (h)

StitcherEase: Make a quilt center of Delectable Mountains or blocks of leaves or trees; then border it with this design, embroidered in different colors for different seasons. "Mist" lines may range through grays and blues to white.

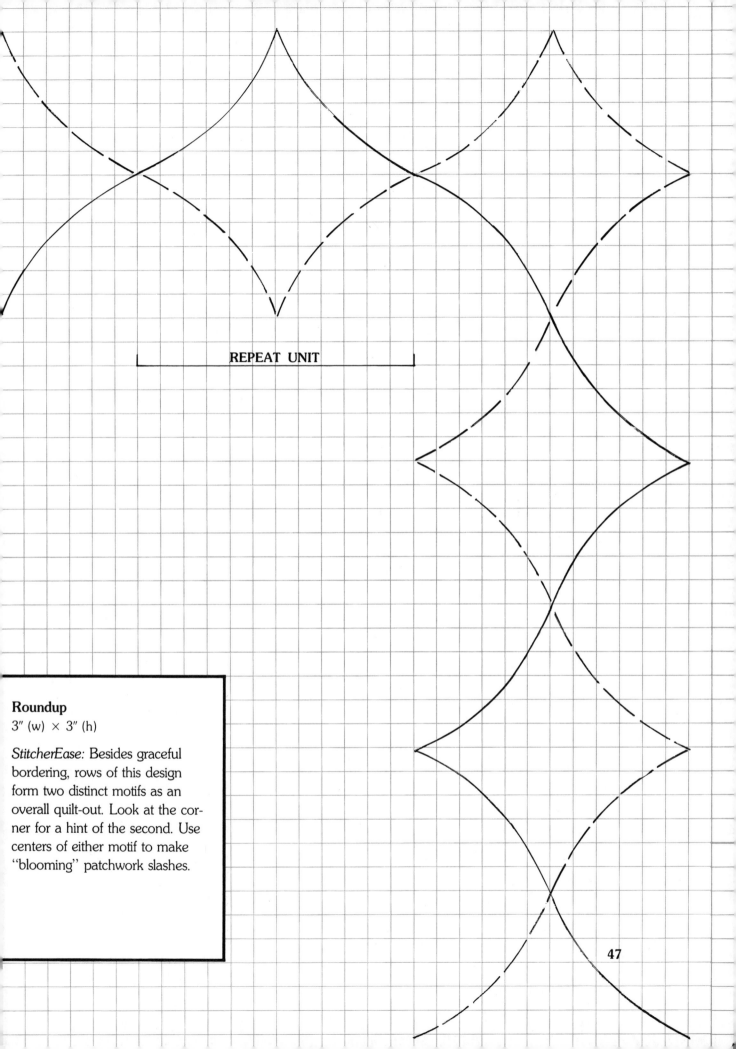

REPEAT UNIT

Roundup
3″ (w) × 3″ (h)

StitcherEase: Besides graceful bordering, rows of this design form two distinct motifs as an overall quilt-out. Look at the corner for a hint of the second. Use centers of either motif to make "blooming" patchwork slashes.

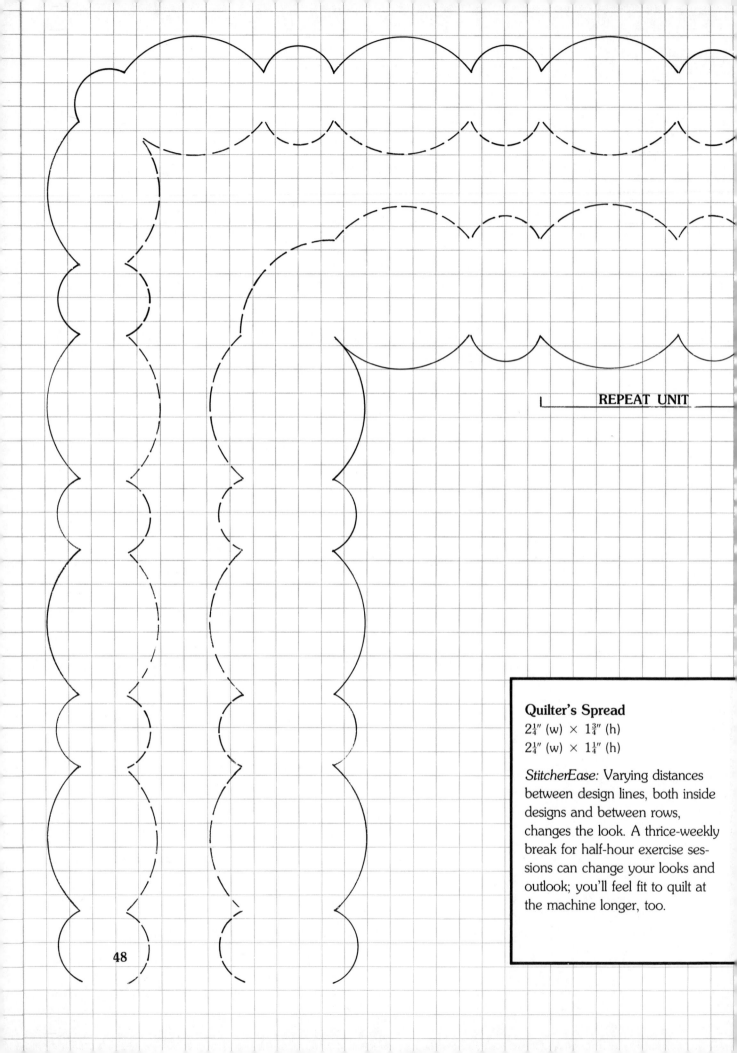

REPEAT UNIT

Quilter's Spread
$2\frac{1}{4}''$ (w) $\times$ $1\frac{3}{4}''$ (h)
$2\frac{1}{4}''$ (w) $\times$ $1\frac{1}{4}''$ (h)

StitcherEase: Varying distances between design lines, both inside designs and between rows, changes the look. A thrice-weekly break for half-hour exercise sessions can change your looks and outlook; you'll feel fit to quilt at the machine longer, too.

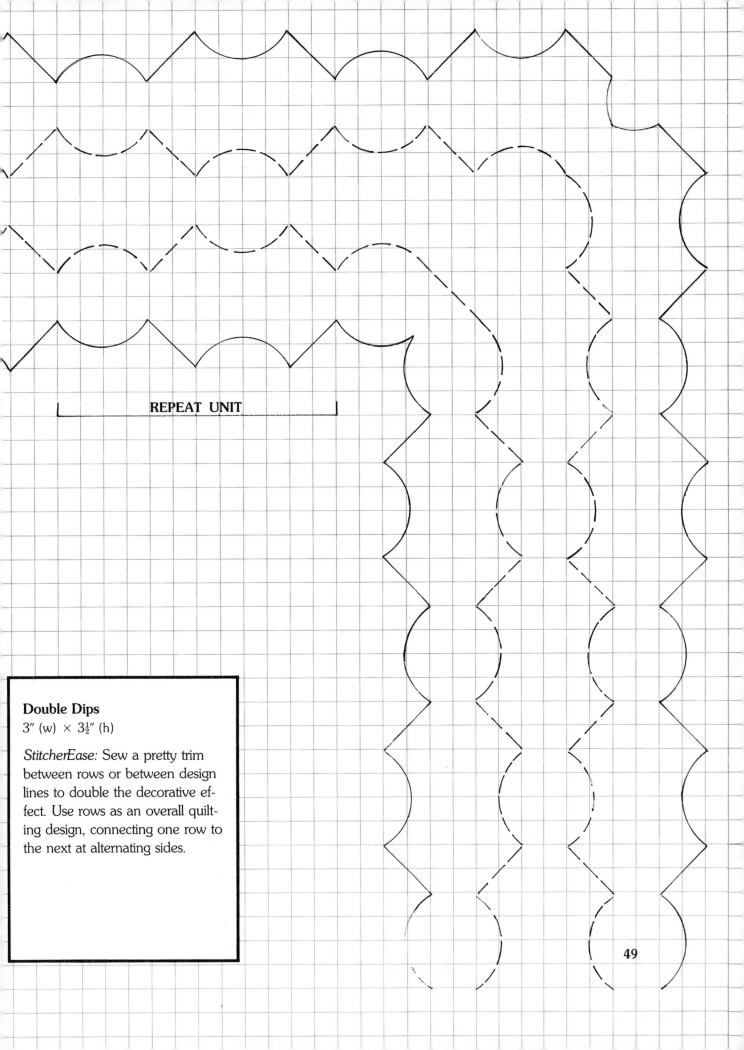

REPEAT UNIT

Double Dips
3″ (w) × 3½″ (h)

StitcherEase: Sew a pretty trim between rows or between design lines to double the decorative effect. Use rows as an overall quilting design, connecting one row to the next at alternating sides.

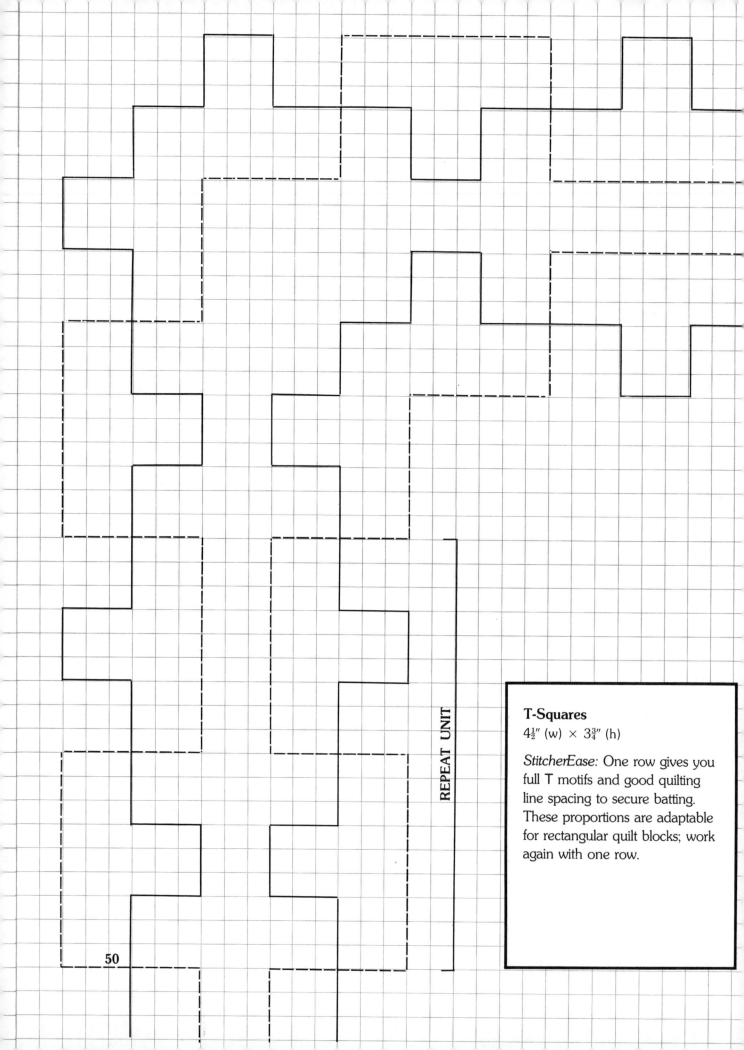

REPEAT UNIT

T-Squares

$4\frac{1}{2}''$ (w) $\times$ $3\frac{3}{4}''$ (h)

StitcherEase: One row gives you full **T** motifs and good quilting line spacing to secure batting. These proportions are adaptable for rectangular quilt blocks; work again with one row.

50

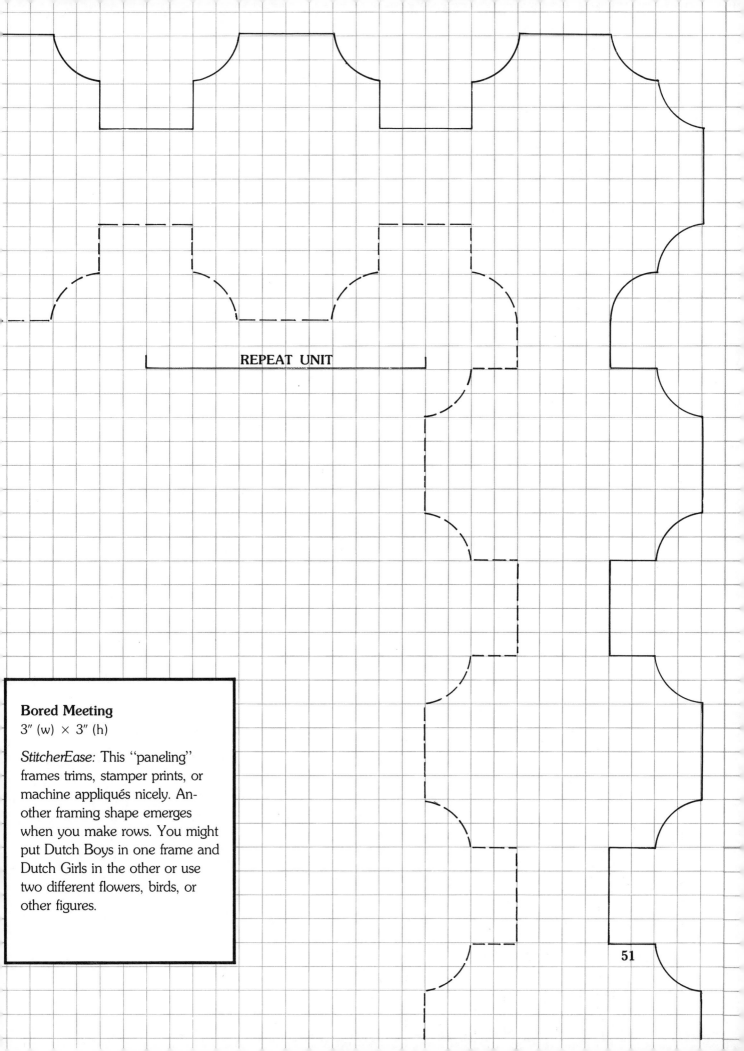

REPEAT UNIT

Bored Meeting
3″ (w) × 3″ (h)

StitcherEase: This "paneling" frames trims, stamper prints, or machine appliqués nicely. Another framing shape emerges when you make rows. You might put Dutch Boys in one frame and Dutch Girls in the other or use two different flowers, birds, or other figures.

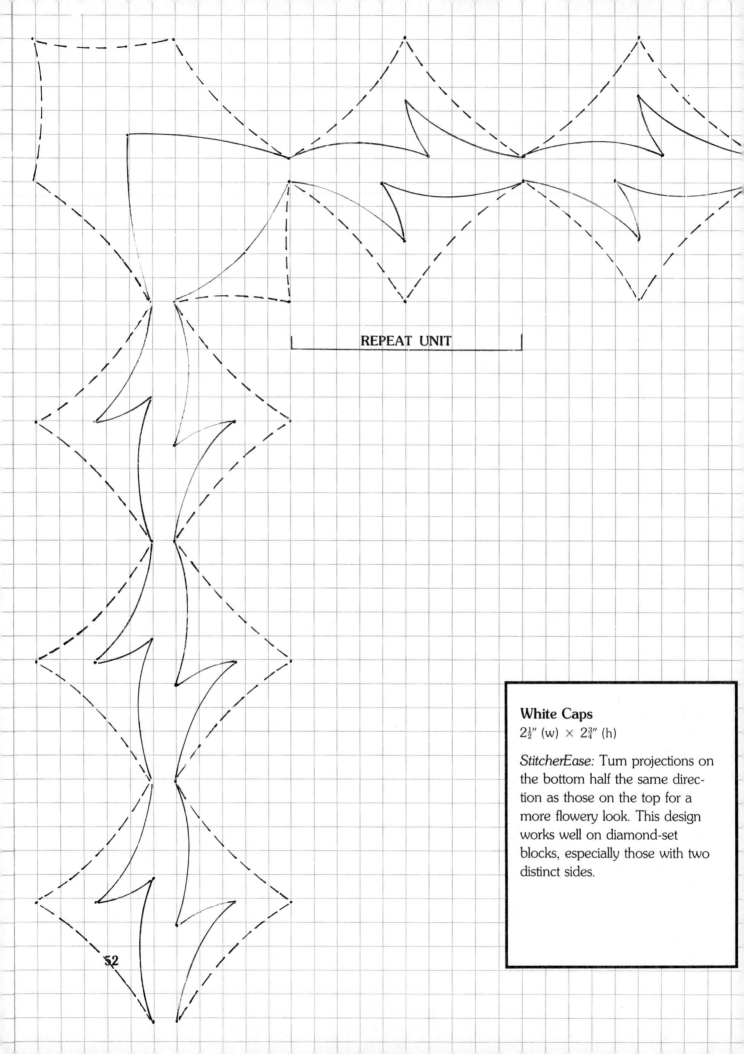

REPEAT UNIT

White Caps

$2\frac{1}{2}''$ (w) × $2\frac{3}{4}''$ (h)

StitcherEase: Turn projections on the bottom half the same direction as those on the top for a more flowery look. This design works well on diamond-set blocks, especially those with two distinct sides.

52

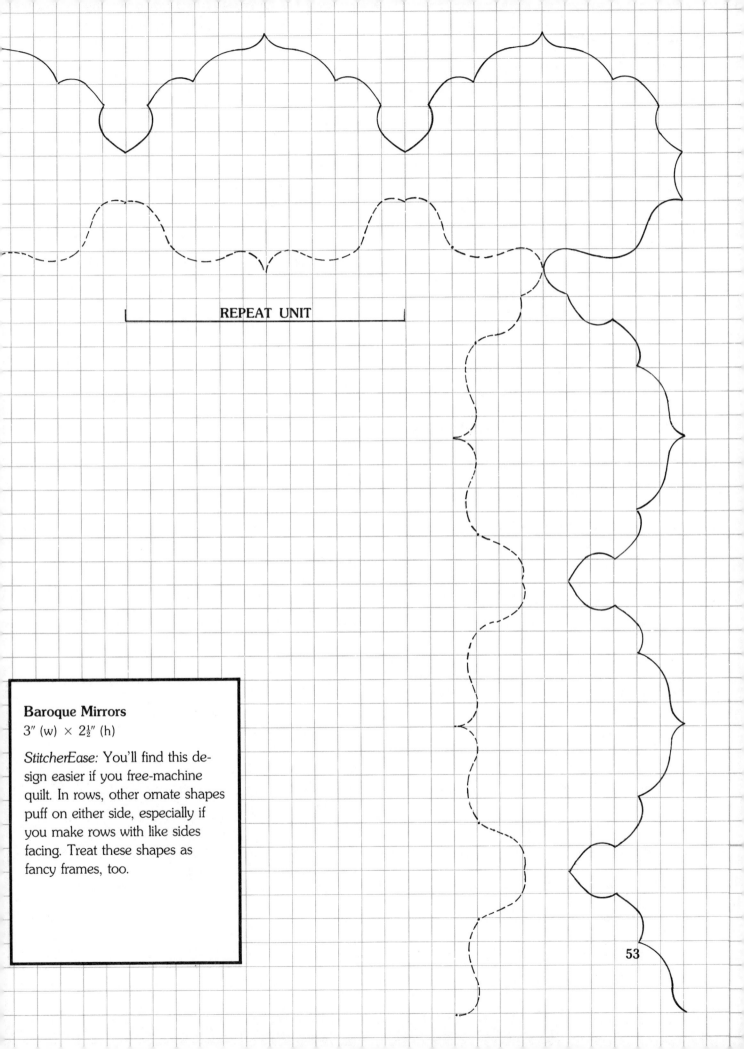

REPEAT UNIT

Baroque Mirrors
3″ (w) × 2½″ (h)

StitcherEase: You'll find this design easier if you free-machine quilt. In rows, other ornate shapes puff on either side, especially if you make rows with like sides facing. Treat these shapes as fancy frames, too.

53

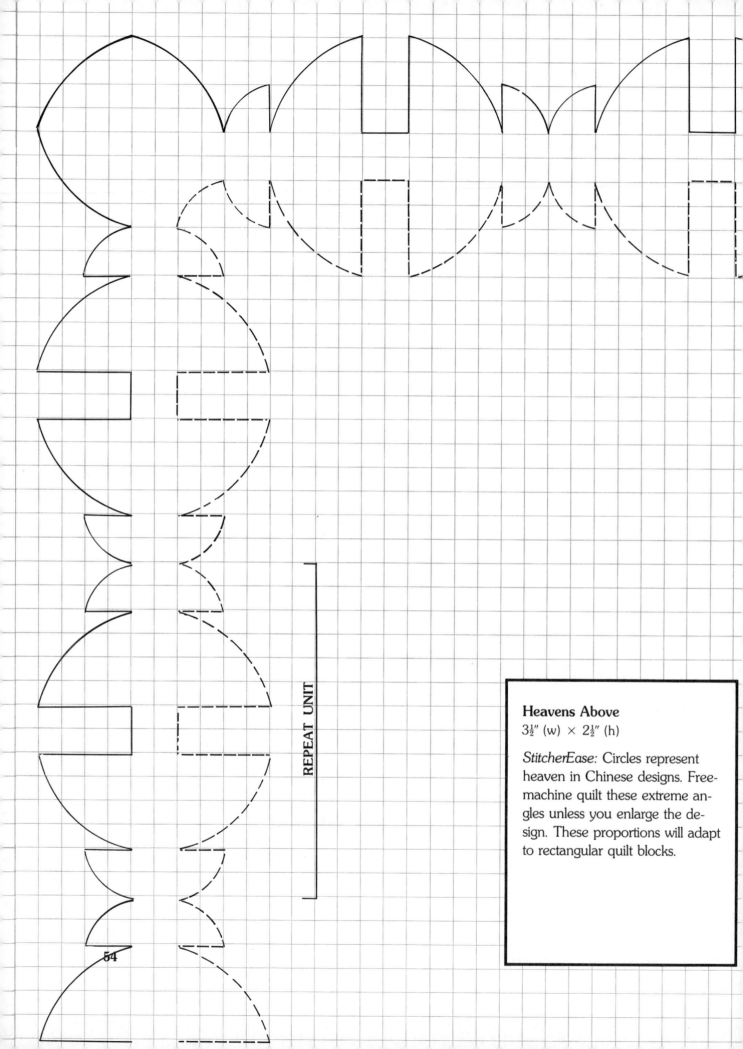

REPEAT UNIT

54

Heavens Above
$3\frac{1}{2}''$ (w) $\times$ $2\frac{1}{2}''$ (h)

StitcherEase: Circles represent heaven in Chinese designs. Free-machine quilt these extreme angles unless you enlarge the design. These proportions will adapt to rectangular quilt blocks.

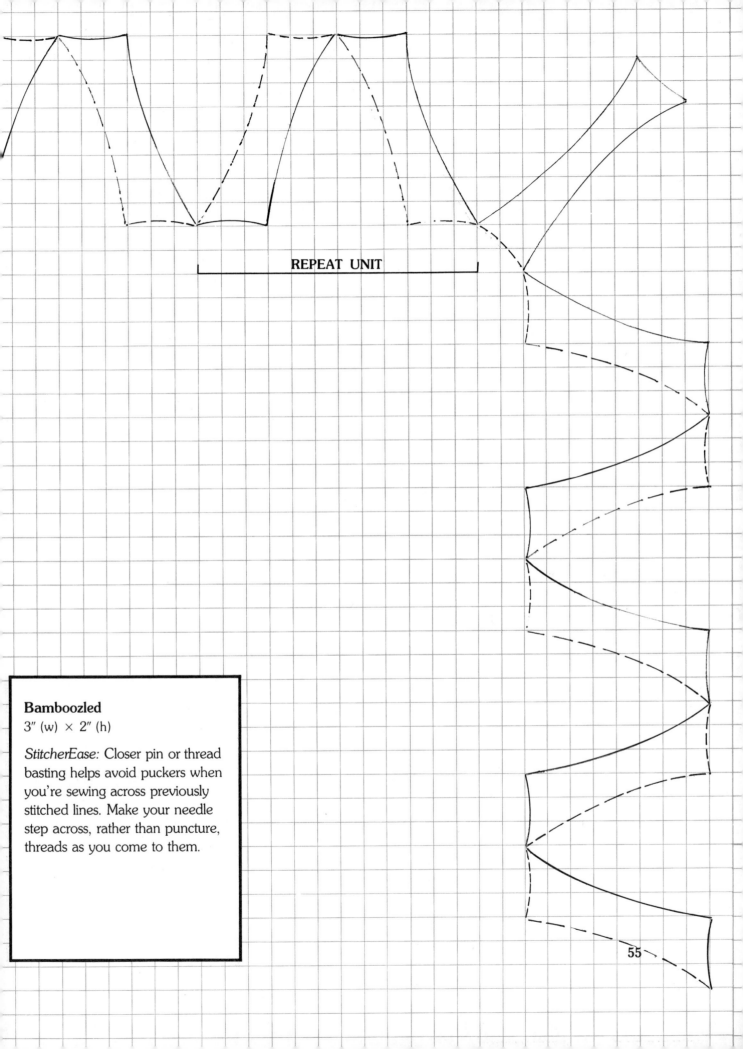

REPEAT UNIT

Bamboozled

3″ (w) × 2″ (h)

StitcherEase: Closer pin or thread basting helps avoid puckers when you're sewing across previously stitched lines. Make your needle step across, rather than puncture, threads as you come to them.

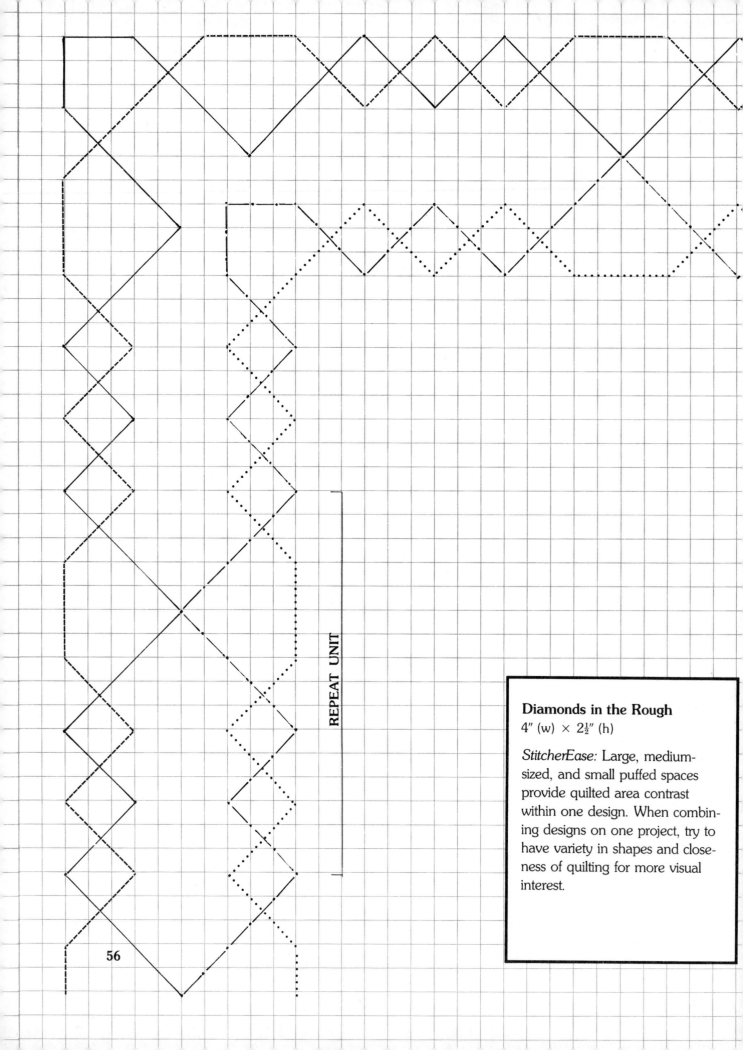

REPEAT UNIT

Diamonds in the Rough
4″ (w) × 2½″ (h)

StitcherEase: Large, medium-sized, and small puffed spaces provide quilted area contrast within one design. When combining designs on one project, try to have variety in shapes and closeness of quilting for more visual interest.

56

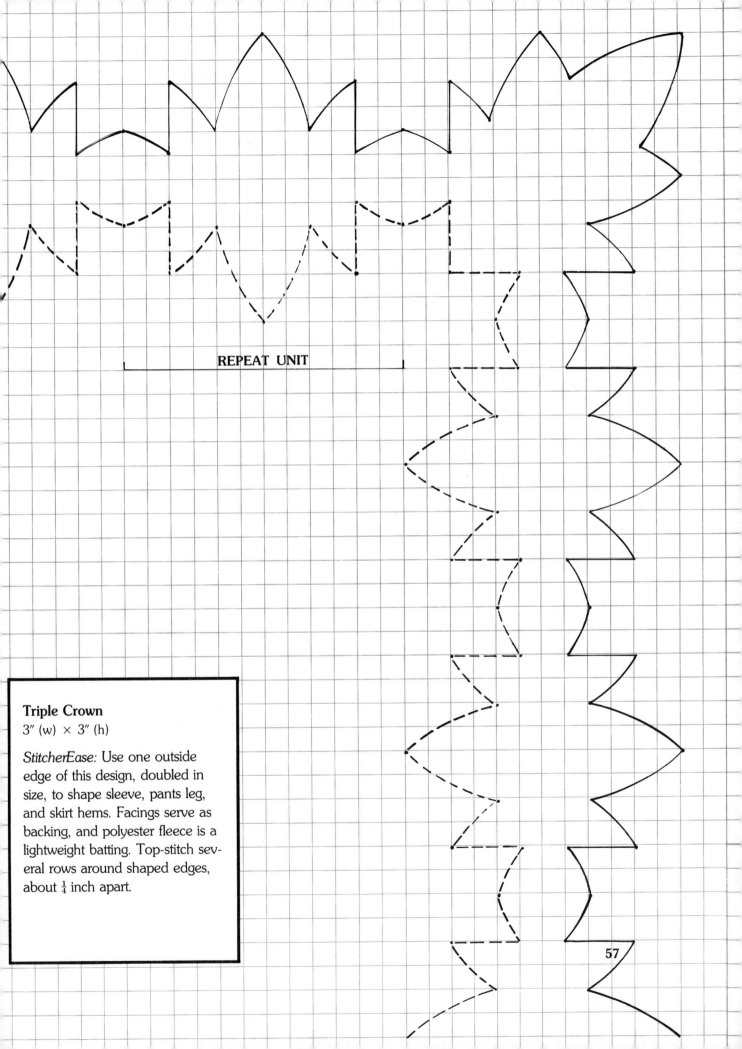

REPEAT UNIT

Triple Crown
3″ (w) × 3″ (h)

StitcherEase: Use one outside edge of this design, doubled in size, to shape sleeve, pants leg, and skirt hems. Facings serve as backing, and polyester fleece is a lightweight batting. Top-stitch several rows around shaped edges, about $\frac{1}{4}$ inch apart.

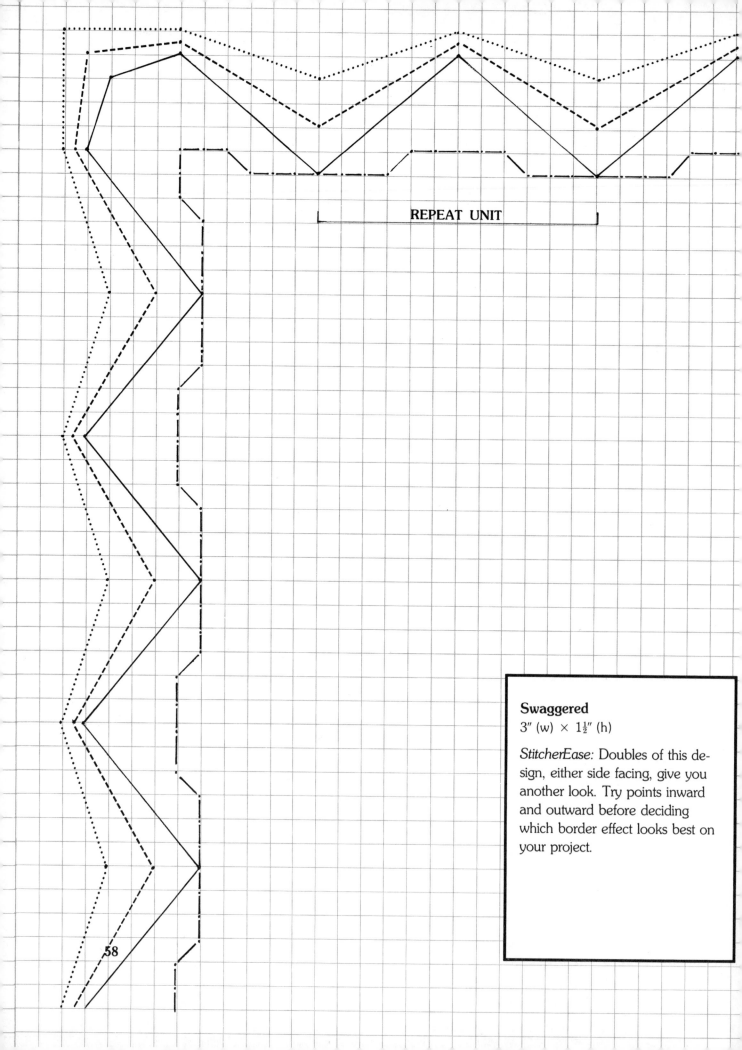

REPEAT UNIT

Swaggered

3″ (w) × 1½″ (h)

StitcherEase: Doubles of this design, either side facing, give you another look. Try points inward and outward before deciding which border effect looks best on your project.

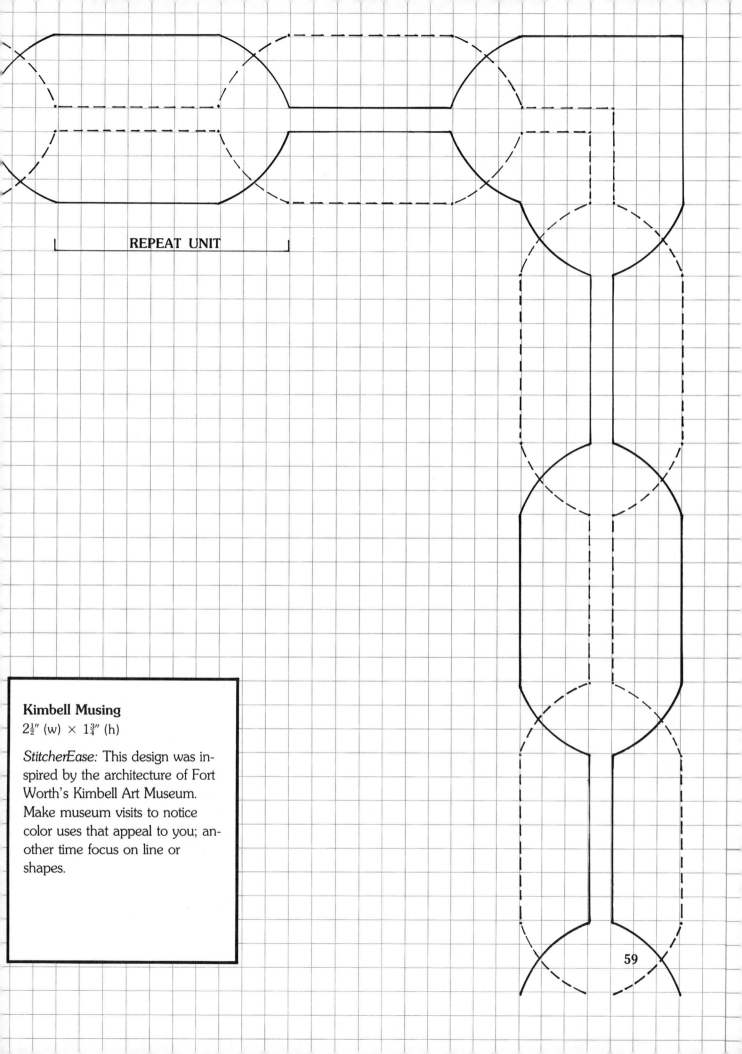

REPEAT UNIT

Kimbell Musing
$2\frac{1}{2}''$ (w) $\times$ $1\frac{3}{4}''$ (h)

StitcherEase: This design was inspired by the architecture of Fort Worth's Kimbell Art Museum. Make museum visits to notice color uses that appeal to you; another time focus on line or shapes.

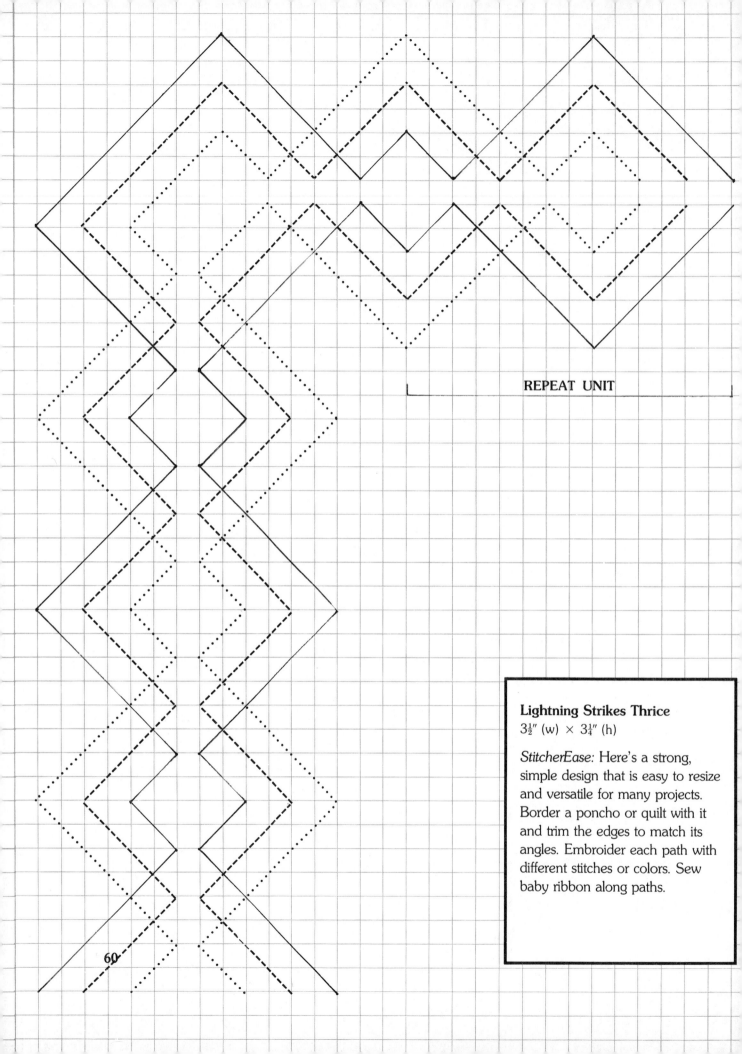

REPEAT UNIT

Lightning Strikes Thrice
$3\frac{1}{2}''$ (w) $\times$ $3\frac{1}{4}''$ (h)

StitcherEase: Here's a strong, simple design that is easy to resize and versatile for many projects. Border a poncho or quilt with it and trim the edges to match its angles. Embroider each path with different stitches or colors. Sew baby ribbon along paths.

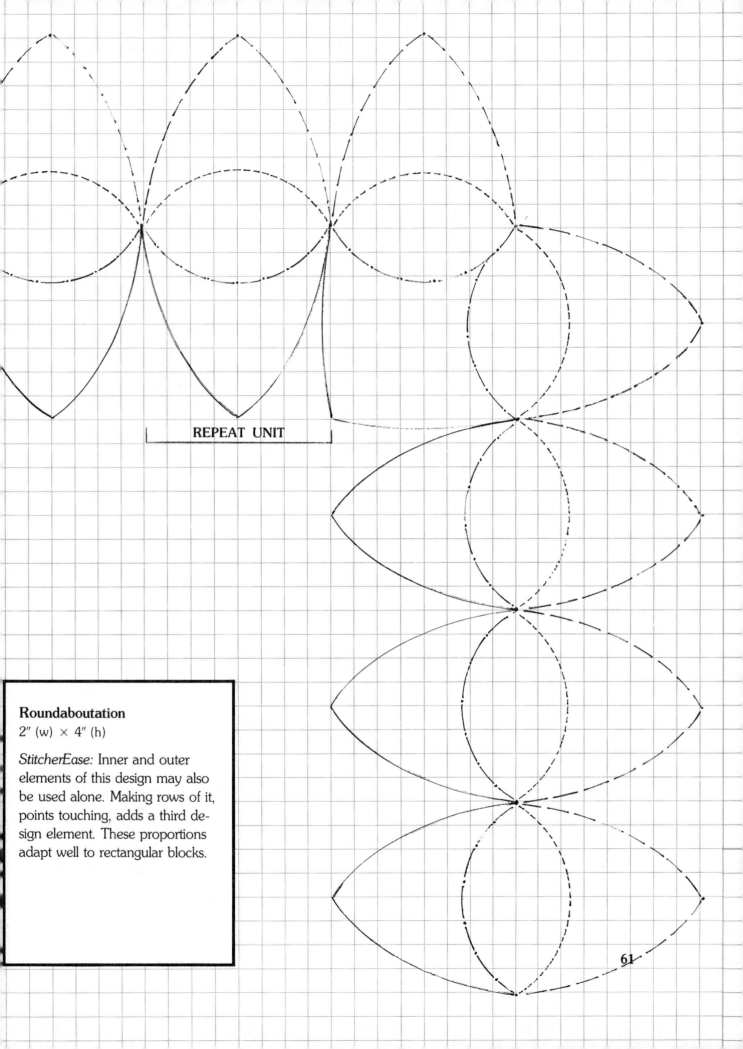

REPEAT UNIT

Roundaboutation

2″ (w) × 4″ (h)

StitcherEase: Inner and outer elements of this design may also be used alone. Making rows of it, points touching, adds a third design element. These proportions adapt well to rectangular blocks.

61

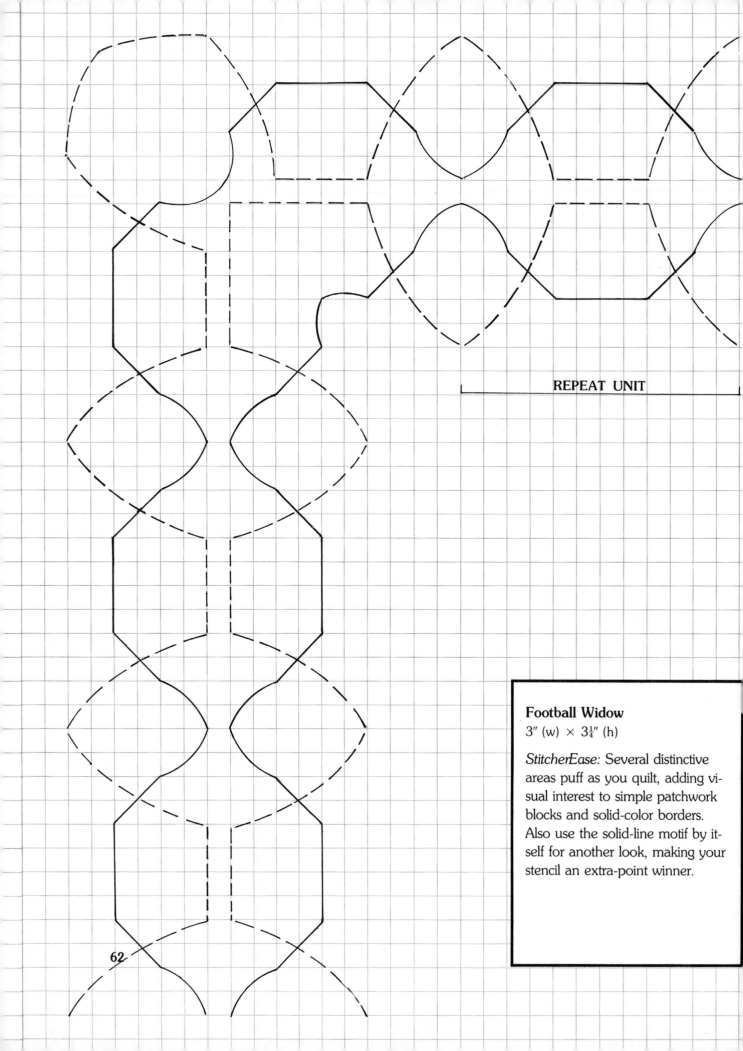

REPEAT UNIT

Football Widow
3″ (w) × 3¼″ (h)

StitcherEase: Several distinctive areas puff as you quilt, adding visual interest to simple patchwork blocks and solid-color borders. Also use the solid-line motif by itself for another look, making your stencil an extra-point winner.

62

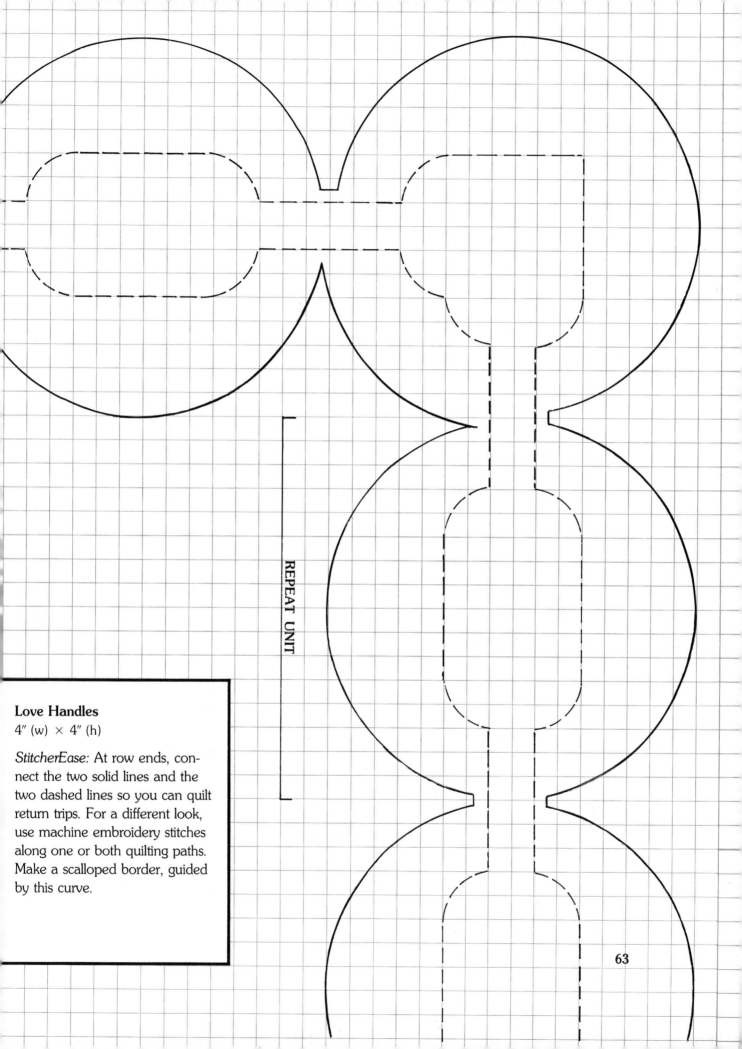

Love Handles
4″ (w) × 4″ (h)

StitcherEase: At row ends, connect the two solid lines and the two dashed lines so you can quilt return trips. For a different look, use machine embroidery stitches along one or both quilting paths. Make a scalloped border, guided by this curve.

REPEAT UNIT

63

REPEAT UNIT

64

Dilly Dahlias
6″ (w) × 3″ (h)

StitcherEase: Only free-machine quilting will put these posies on your projects with carefree grace. Use a very narrow zig-zag stitch, and remember that free-machine quilting isn't meant to have the more rigid perfection of presser-foot quilting—that's part of its charm.

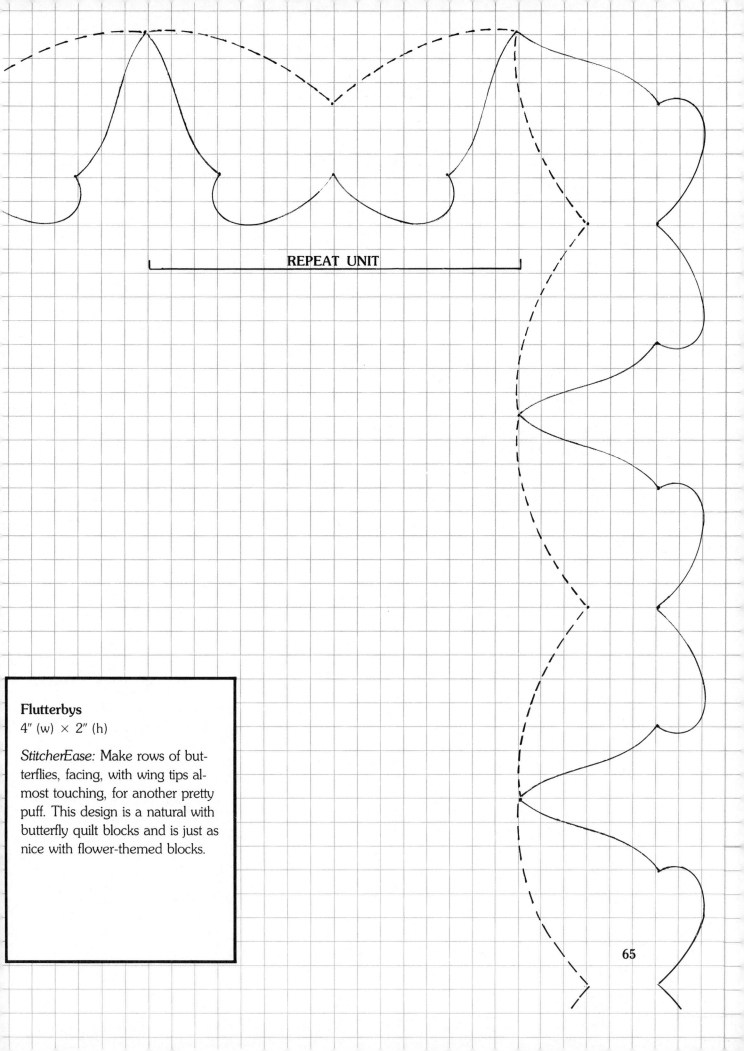

REPEAT UNIT

Flutterbys
4″ (w) × 2″ (h)

StitcherEase: Make rows of butterflies, facing, with wing tips almost touching, for another pretty puff. This design is a natural with butterfly quilt blocks and is just as nice with flower-themed blocks.

65

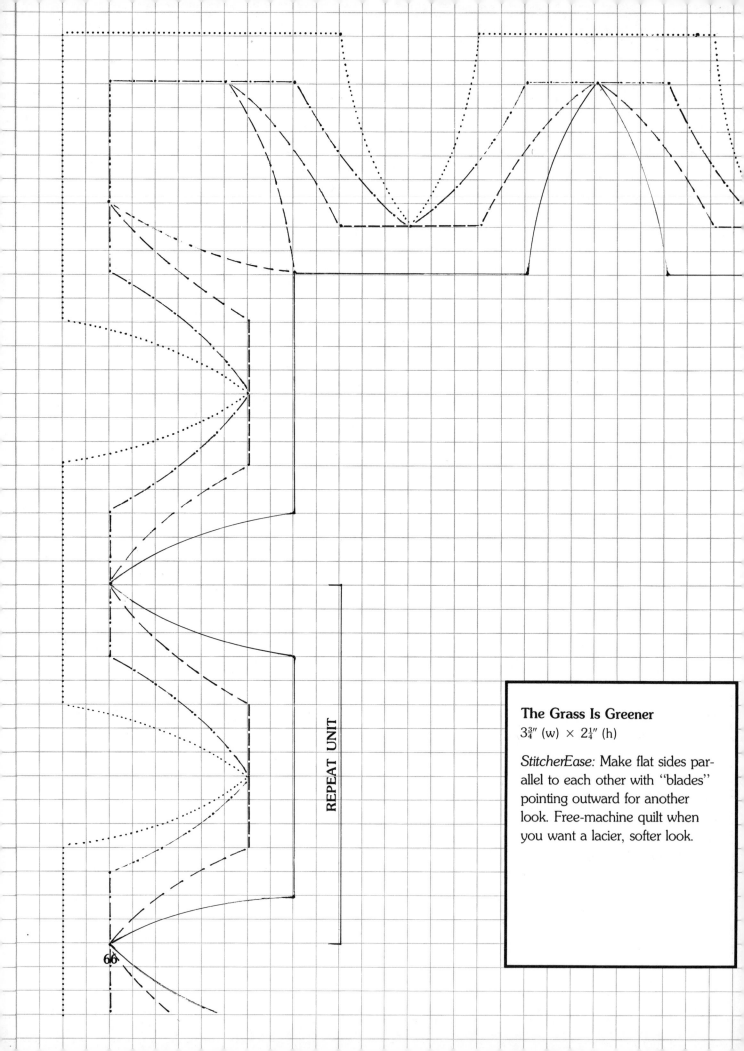

REPEAT UNIT

The Grass Is Greener

$3\frac{3}{4}''$ (w) $\times$ $2\frac{1}{4}''$ (h)

StitcherEase: Make flat sides parallel to each other with ''blades'' pointing outward for another look. Free-machine quilt when you want a lacier, softer look.

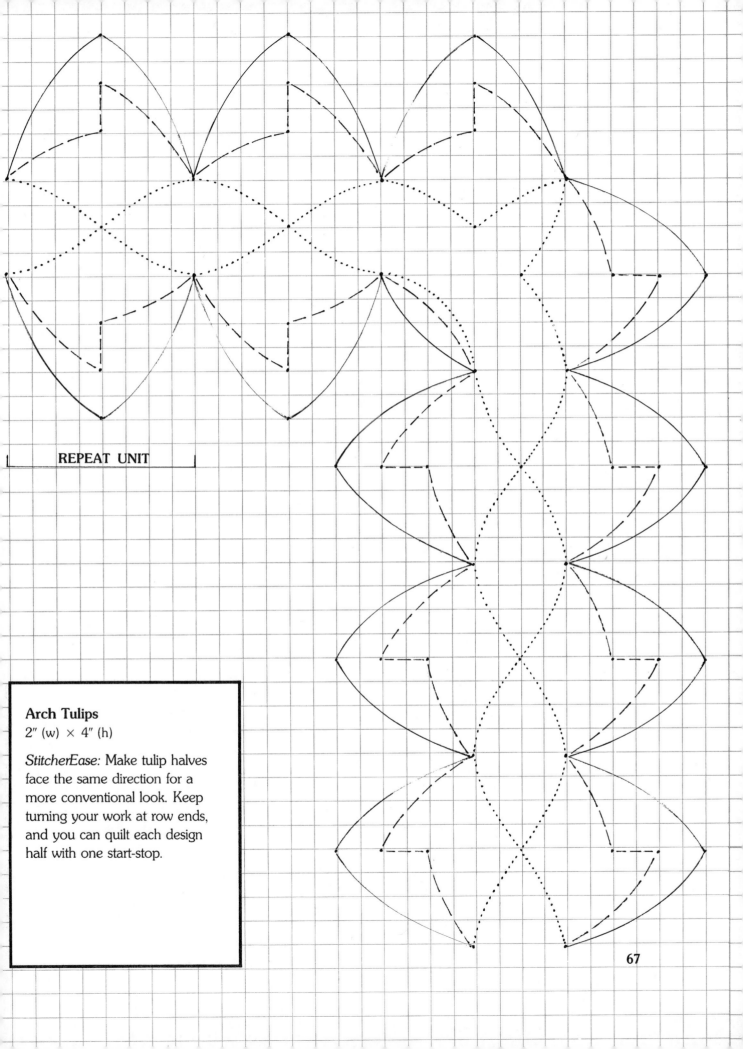

REPEAT UNIT

Arch Tulips

2″ (w) × 4″ (h)

StitcherEase: Make tulip halves face the same direction for a more conventional look. Keep turning your work at row ends, and you can quilt each design half with one start-stop.

67

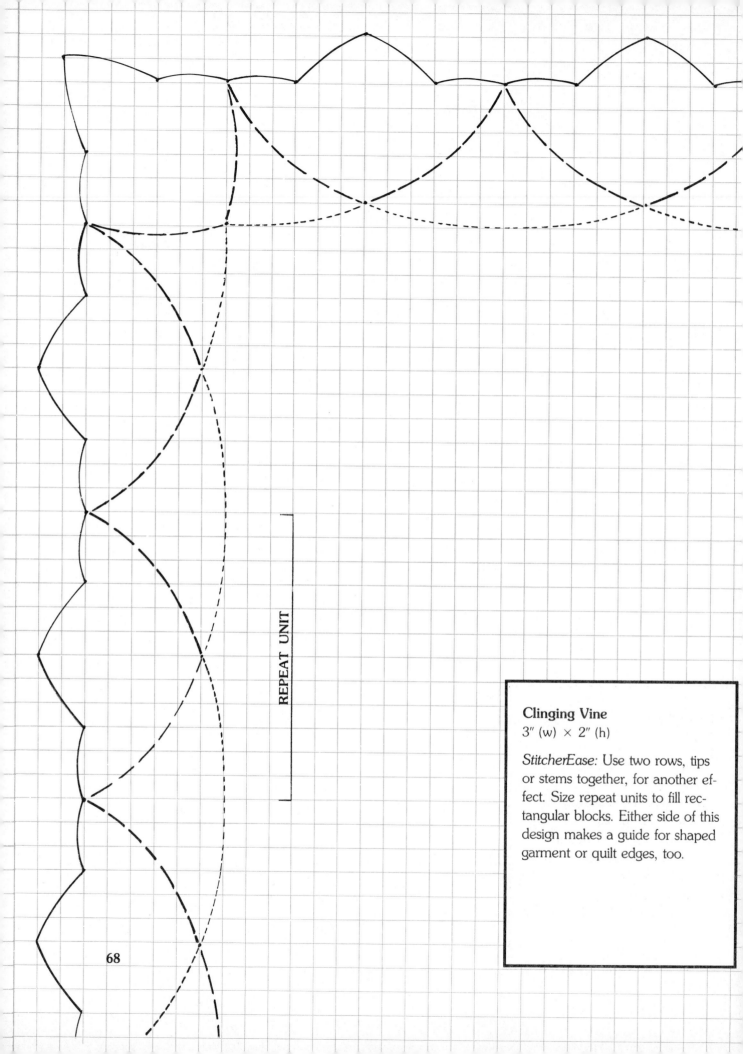

REPEAT UNIT

Clinging Vine
3″ (w) × 2″ (h)

StitcherEase: Use two rows, tips or stems together, for another effect. Size repeat units to fill rectangular blocks. Either side of this design makes a guide for shaped garment or quilt edges, too.

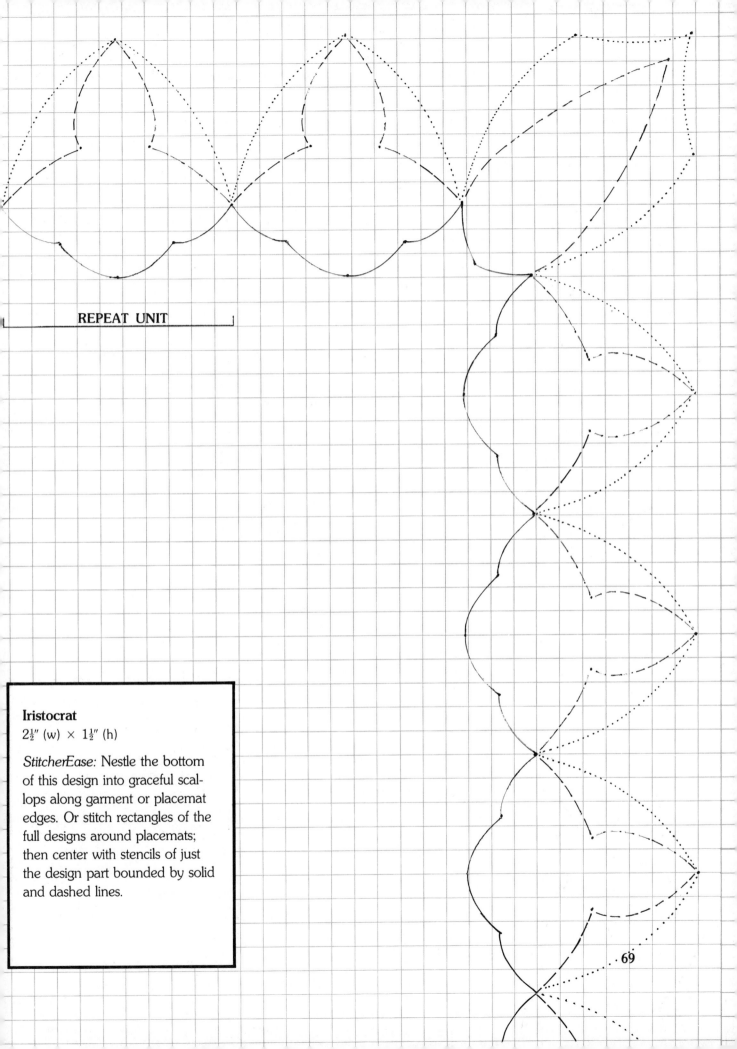

REPEAT UNIT

Iristocrat
$2\frac{1}{2}''$ (w) × $1\frac{1}{2}''$ (h)

StitcherEase: Nestle the bottom of this design into graceful scallops along garment or placemat edges. Or stitch rectangles of the full designs around placemats; then center with stencils of just the design part bounded by solid and dashed lines.

69

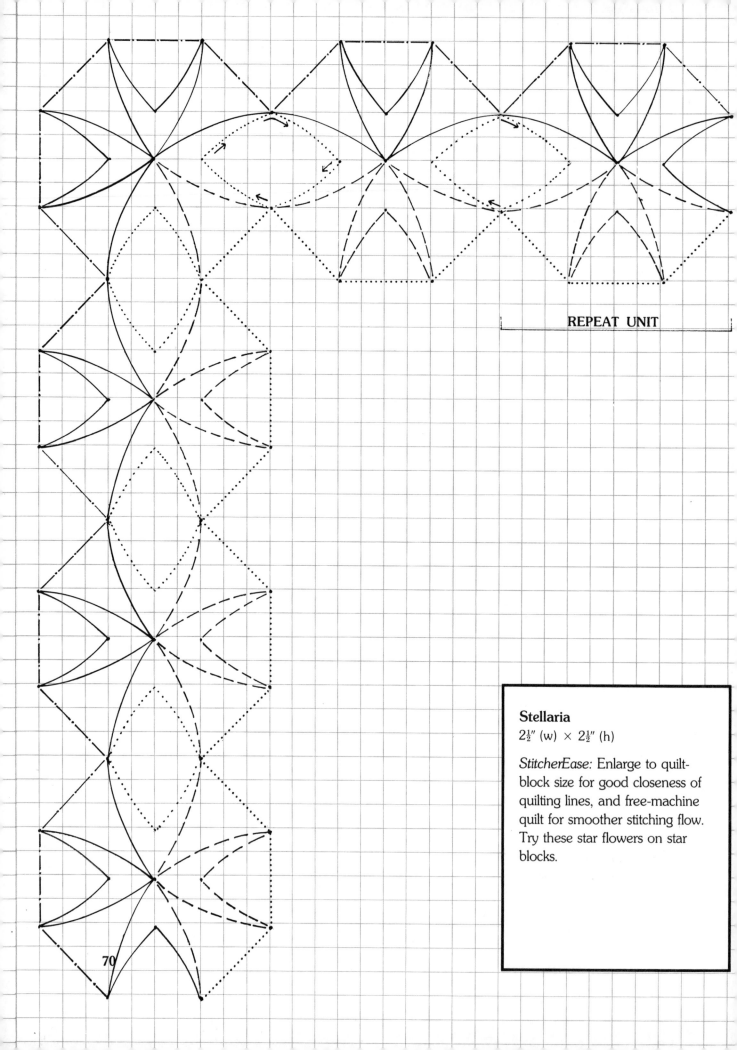

REPEAT UNIT

Stellaria
$2\frac{1}{2}''$ (w) × $2\frac{1}{2}''$ (h)

StitcherEase: Enlarge to quilt-block size for good closeness of quilting lines, and free-machine quilt for smoother stitching flow. Try these star flowers on star blocks.

70

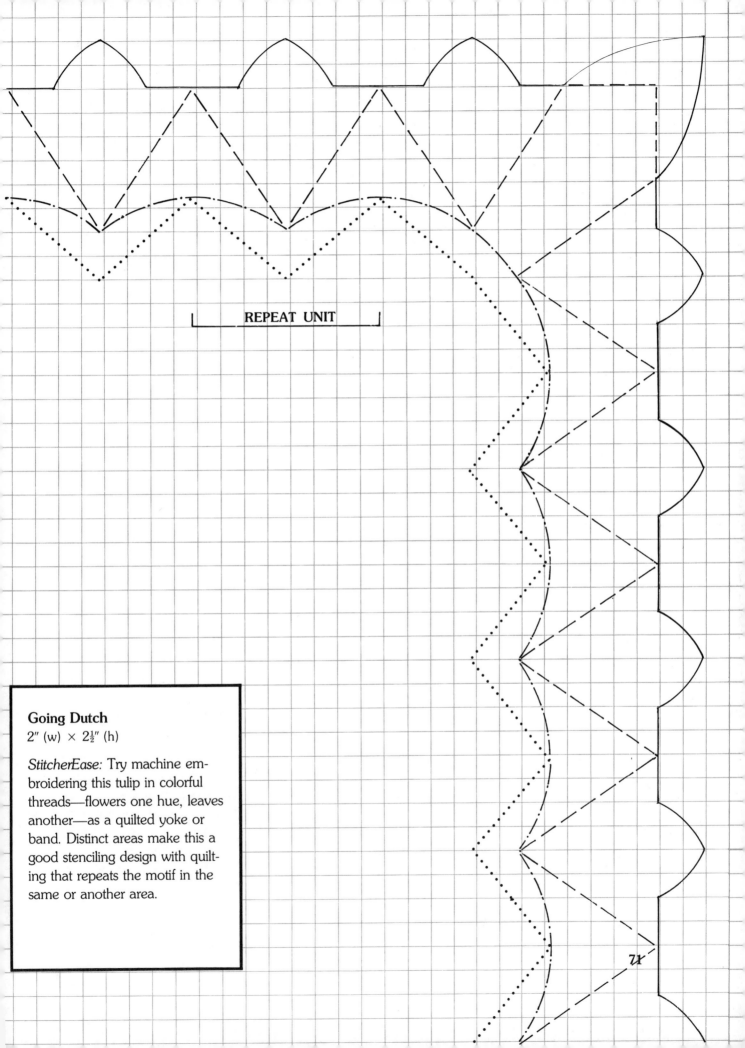

REPEAT UNIT

Going Dutch
2″ (w) × 2½″ (h)

StitcherEase: Try machine embroidering this tulip in colorful threads—flowers one hue, leaves another—as a quilted yoke or band. Distinct areas make this a good stenciling design with quilting that repeats the motif in the same or another area.

71

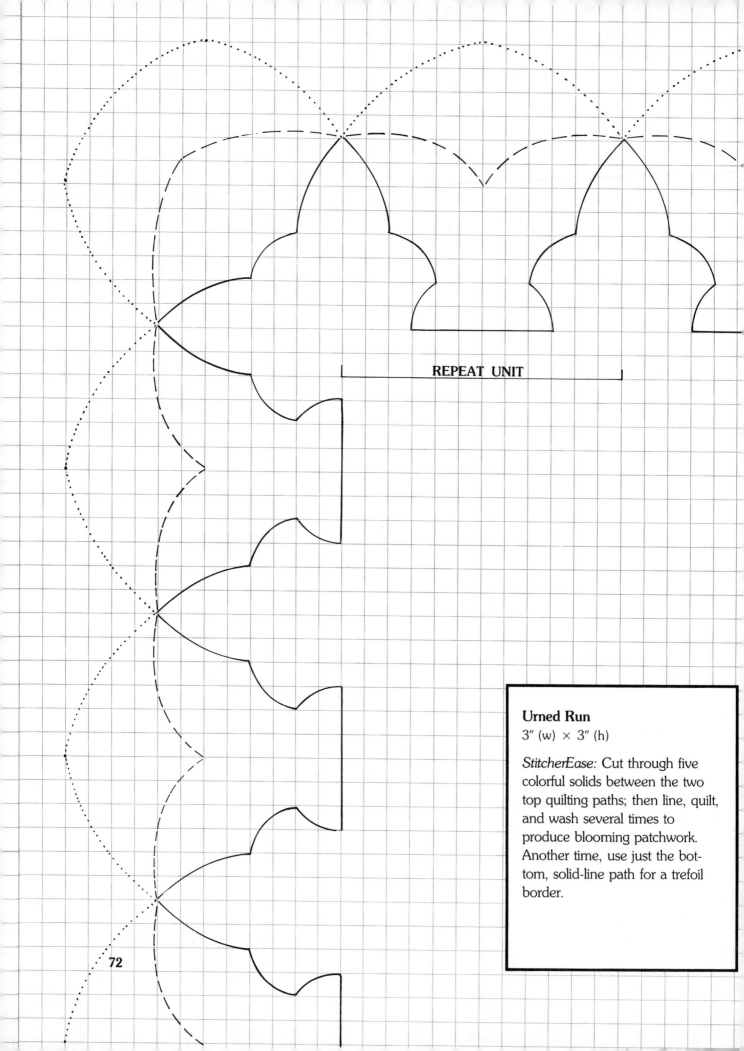

REPEAT UNIT

Urned Run
3″ (w) × 3″ (h)

StitcherEase: Cut through five colorful solids between the two top quilting paths; then line, quilt, and wash several times to produce blooming patchwork. Another time, use just the bottom, solid-line path for a trefoil border.

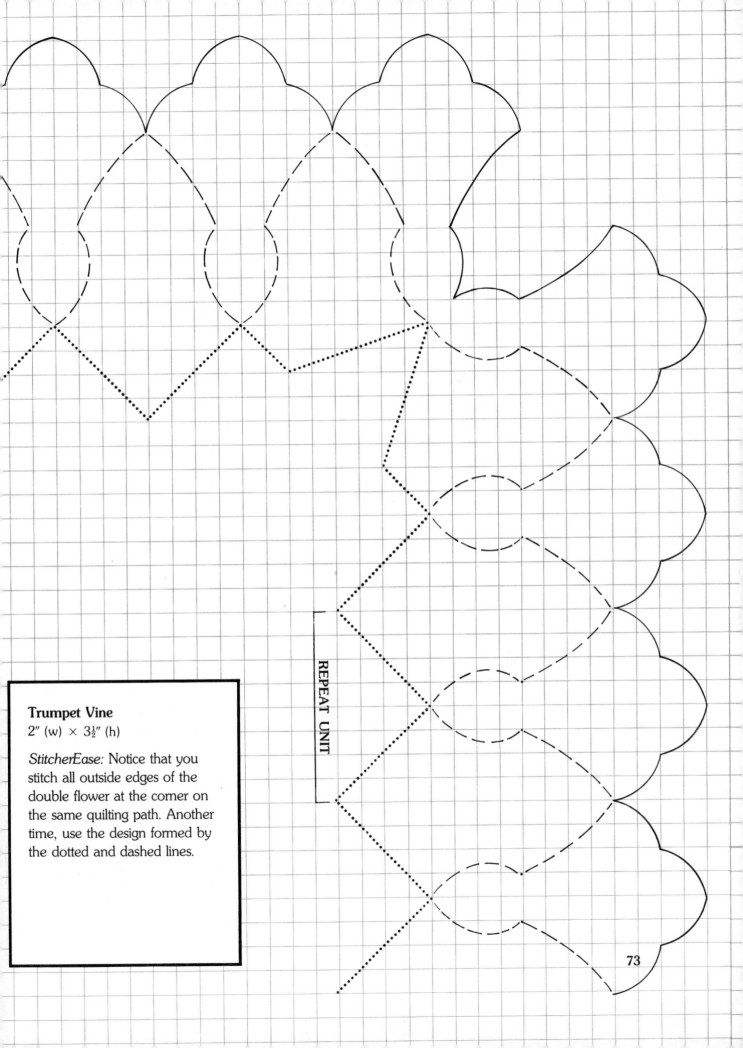

Trumpet Vine

2″ (w) × 3½″ (h)

StitcherEase: Notice that you stitch all outside edges of the double flower at the corner on the same quilting path. Another time, use the design formed by the dotted and dashed lines.

REPEAT UNIT

73

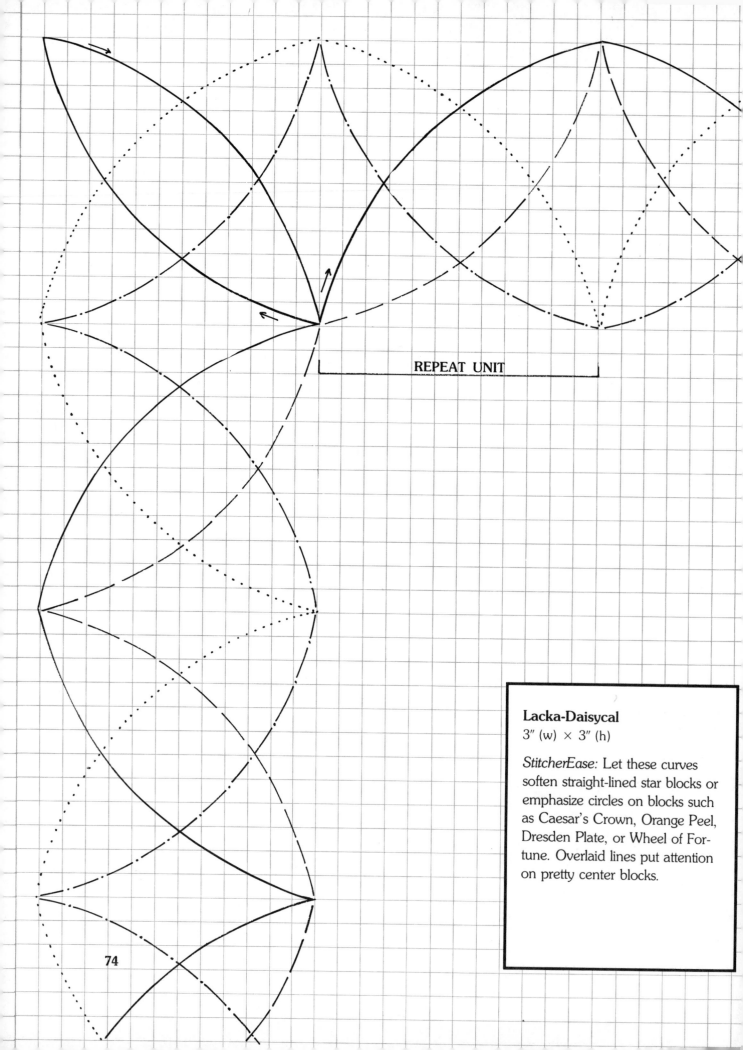

REPEAT UNIT

Lacka-Daisycal
3″ (w) × 3″ (h)

StitcherEase: Let these curves soften straight-lined star blocks or emphasize circles on blocks such as Caesar's Crown, Orange Peel, Dresden Plate, or Wheel of Fortune. Overlaid lines put attention on pretty center blocks.

74

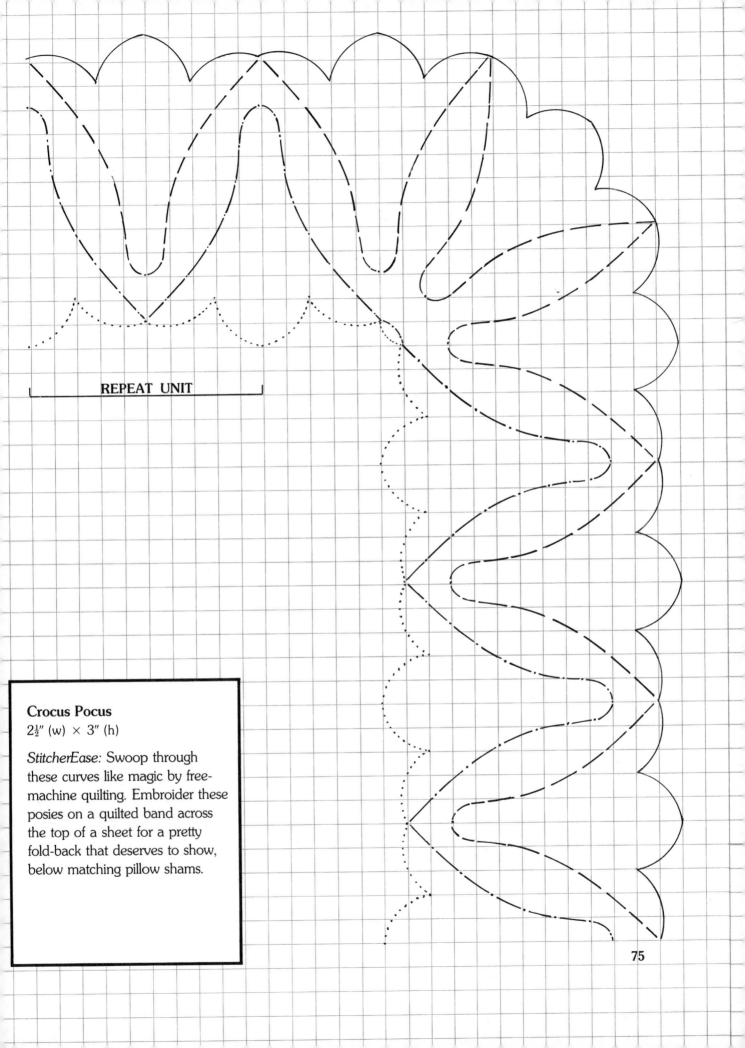

REPEAT UNIT

Crocus Pocus
2½″ (w) × 3″ (h)

StitcherEase: Swoop through these curves like magic by free-machine quilting. Embroider these posies on a quilted band across the top of a sheet for a pretty fold-back that deserves to show, below matching pillow shams.

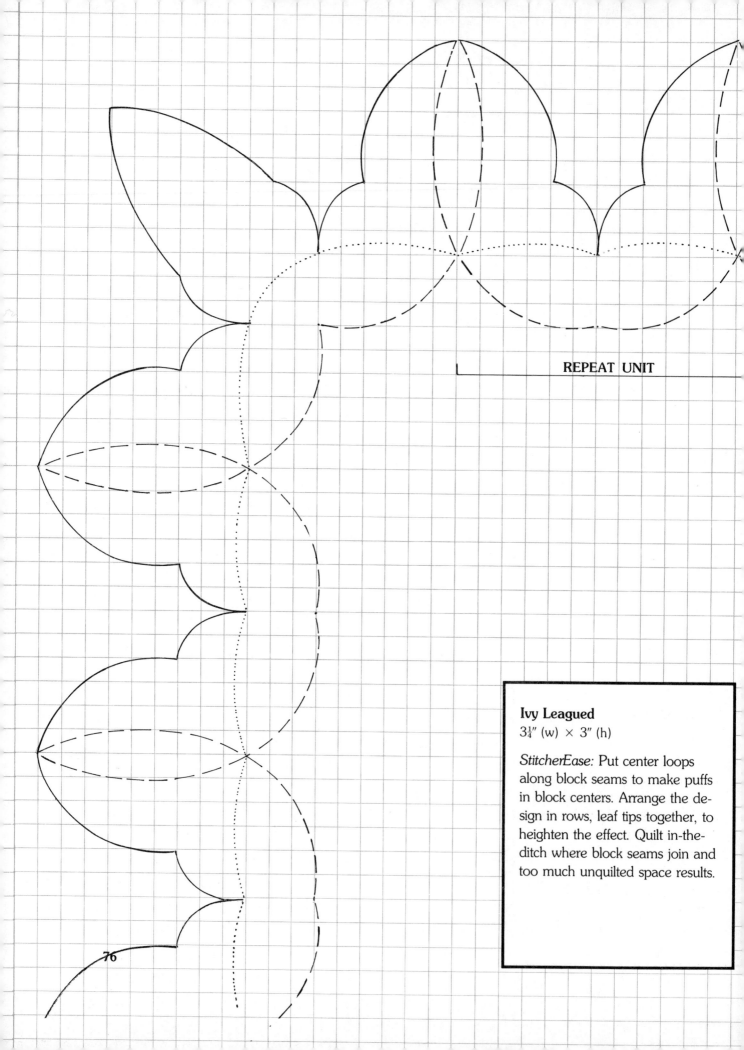

REPEAT UNIT

Ivy Leagued
$3\frac{1}{4}''$ (w) $\times$ 3" (h)

StitcherEase: Put center loops
along block seams to make puffs
in block centers. Arrange the design in rows, leaf tips together, to
heighten the effect. Quilt in-the-
ditch where block seams join and
too much unquilted space results.

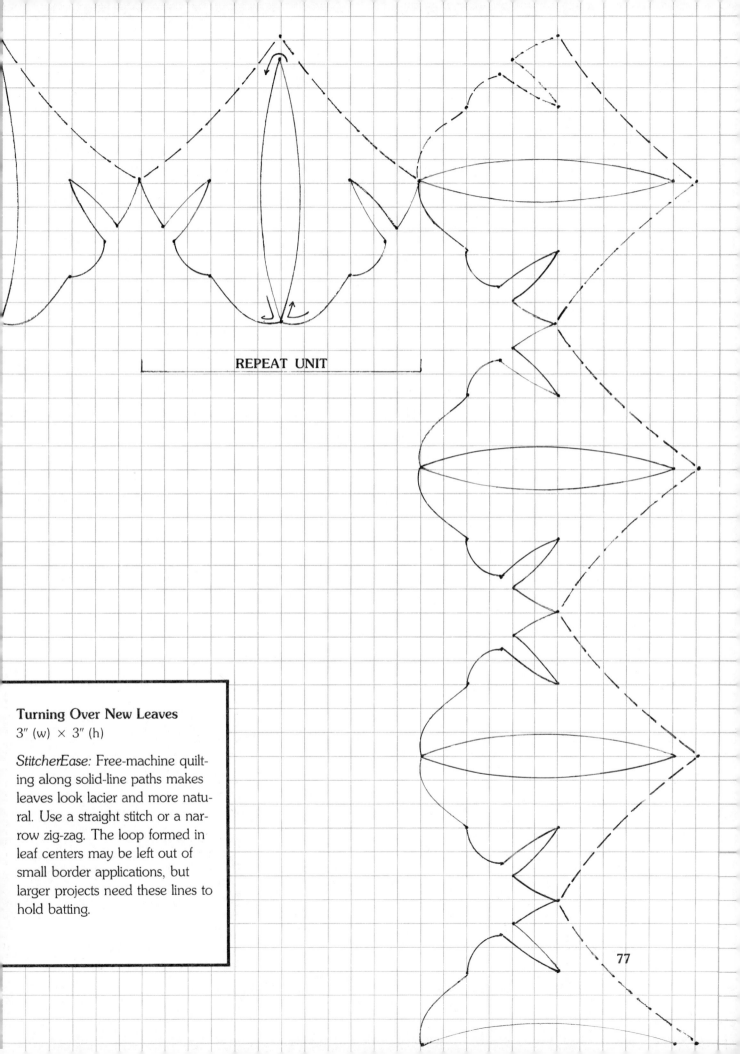

REPEAT UNIT

Turning Over New Leaves
3″ (w) × 3″ (h)

StitcherEase: Free-machine quilting along solid-line paths makes leaves look lacier and more natural. Use a straight stitch or a narrow zig-zag. The loop formed in leaf centers may be left out of small border applications, but larger projects need these lines to hold batting.

77

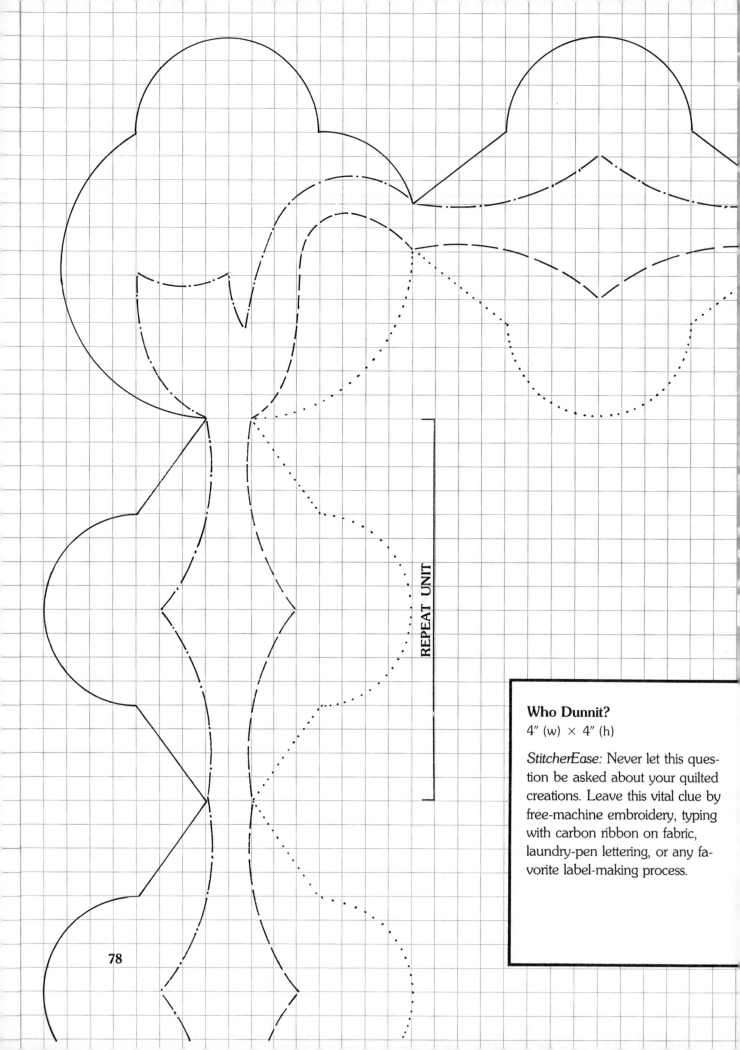

REPEAT UNIT

Who Dunnit?
4″ (w) × 4″ (h)

StitcherEase: Never let this question be asked about your quilted creations. Leave this vital clue by free-machine embroidery, typing with carbon ribbon on fabric, laundry-pen lettering, or any favorite label-making process.

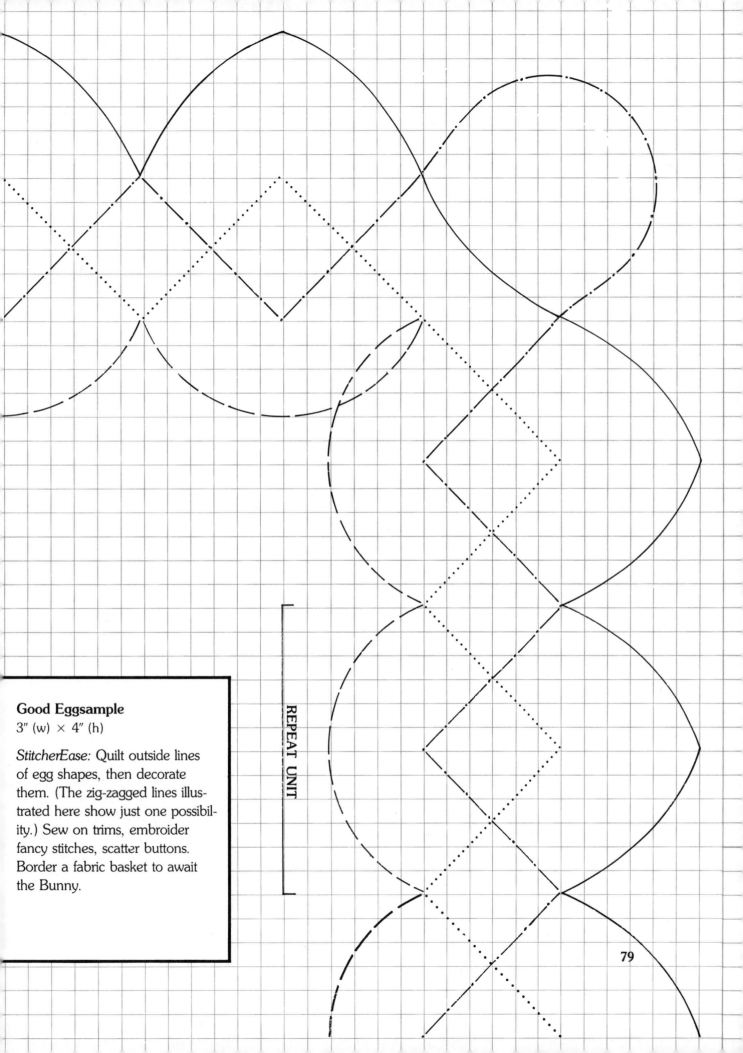

Good Eggsample

3″ (w) × 4″ (h)

StitcherEase: Quilt outside lines of egg shapes, then decorate them. (The zig-zagged lines illustrated here show just one possibility.) Sew on trims, embroider fancy stitches, scatter buttons. Border a fabric basket to await the Bunny.

REPEAT UNIT

79

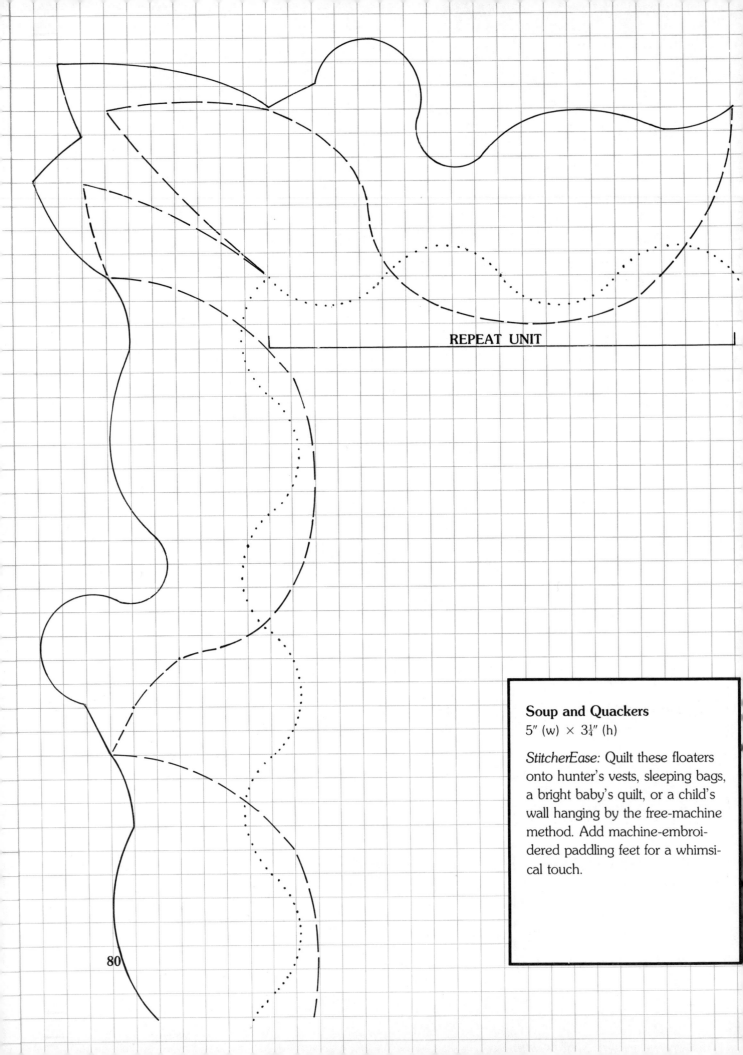

REPEAT UNIT

Soup and Quackers
5″ (w) × 3¼″ (h)

StitcherEase: Quilt these floaters onto hunter's vests, sleeping bags, a bright baby's quilt, or a child's wall hanging by the free-machine method. Add machine-embroidered paddling feet for a whimsical touch.

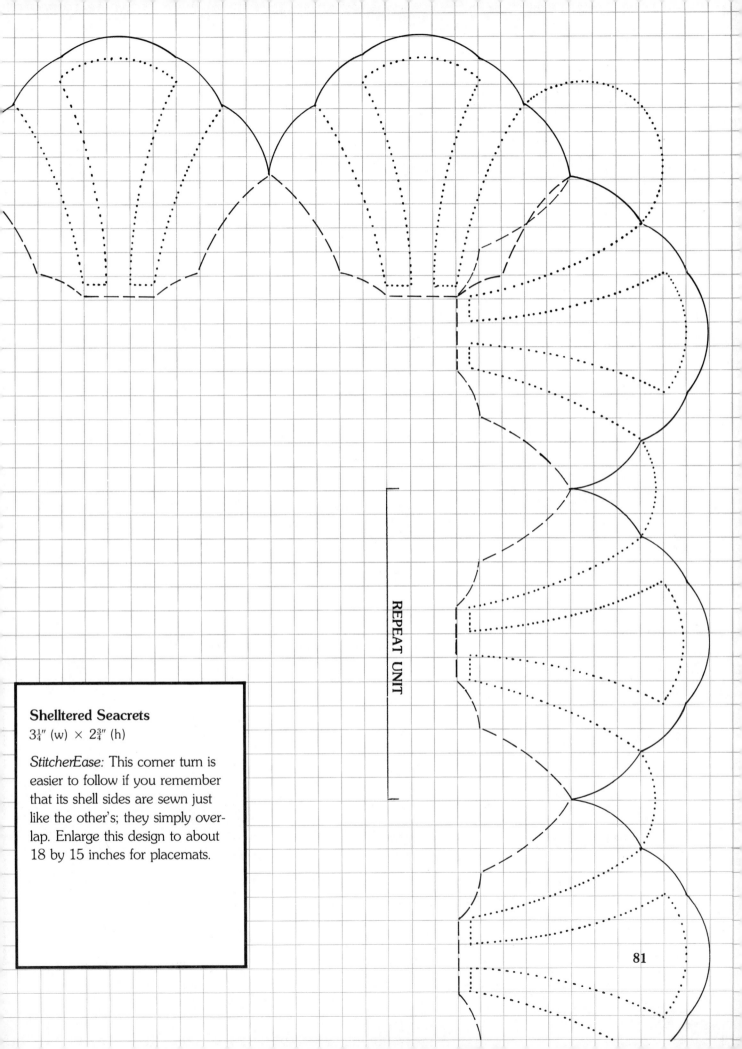

REPEAT UNIT

Shelltered Seacrets

$3\frac{1}{4}''$ (w) $\times$ $2\frac{3}{4}''$ (h)

StitcherEase: This corner turn is easier to follow if you remember that its shell sides are sewn just like the other's; they simply overlap. Enlarge this design to about 18 by 15 inches for placemats.

81

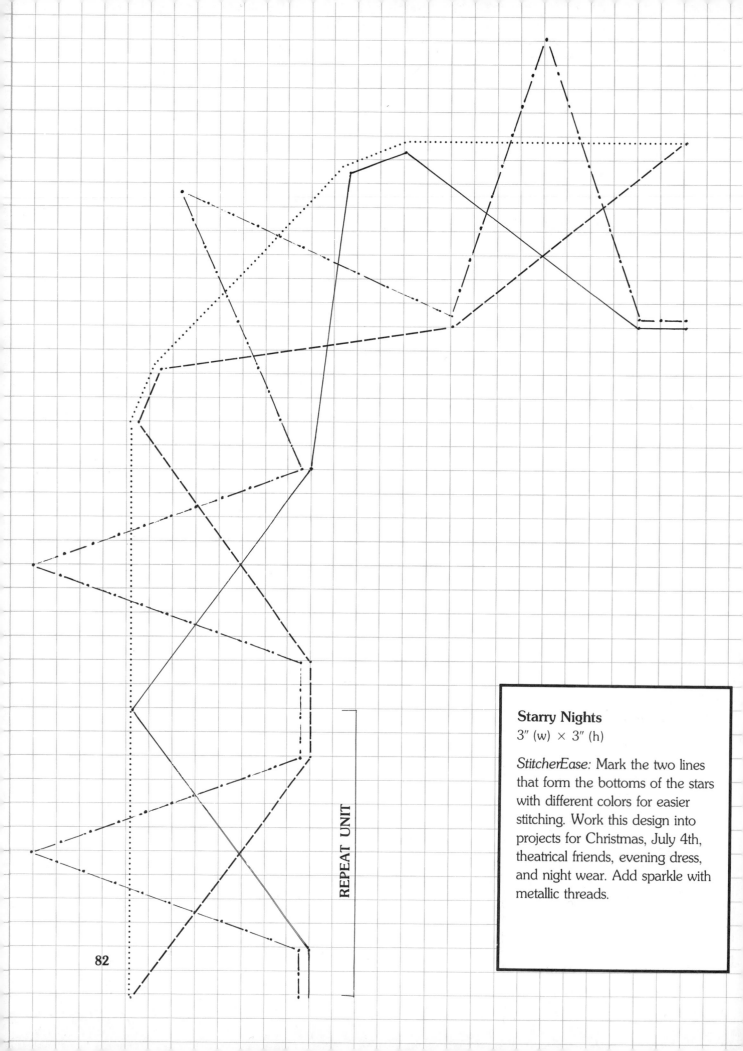

REPEAT UNIT

82

Starry Nights
3″ (w) × 3″ (h)

StitcherEase: Mark the two lines that form the bottoms of the stars with different colors for easier stitching. Work this design into projects for Christmas, July 4th, theatrical friends, evening dress, and night wear. Add sparkle with metallic threads.

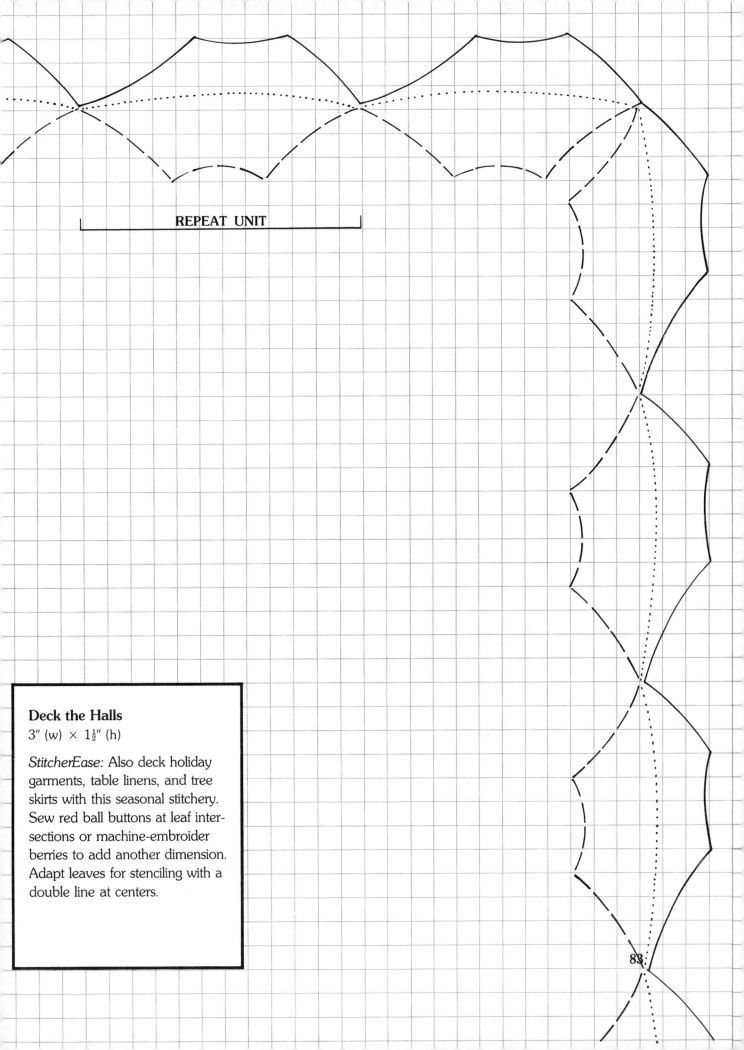

REPEAT UNIT

Deck the Halls

3″ (w) × 1½″ (h)

StitcherEase: Also deck holiday garments, table linens, and tree skirts with this seasonal stitchery. Sew red ball buttons at leaf intersections or machine-embroider berries to add another dimension. Adapt leaves for stenciling with a double line at centers.

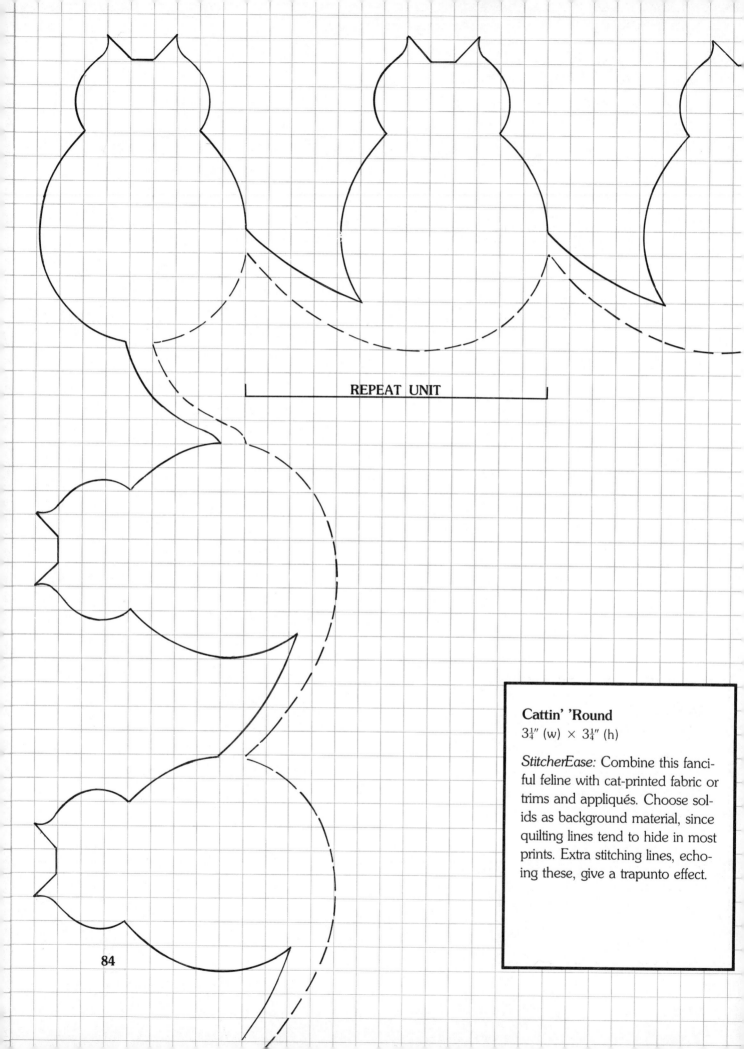

REPEAT UNIT

Cattin' 'Round

$3\frac{1}{4}''$ (w) × $3\frac{1}{4}''$ (h)

StitcherEase: Combine this fanciful feline with cat-printed fabric or trims and appliqués. Choose solids as background material, since quilting lines tend to hide in most prints. Extra stitching lines, echoing these, give a trapunto effect.

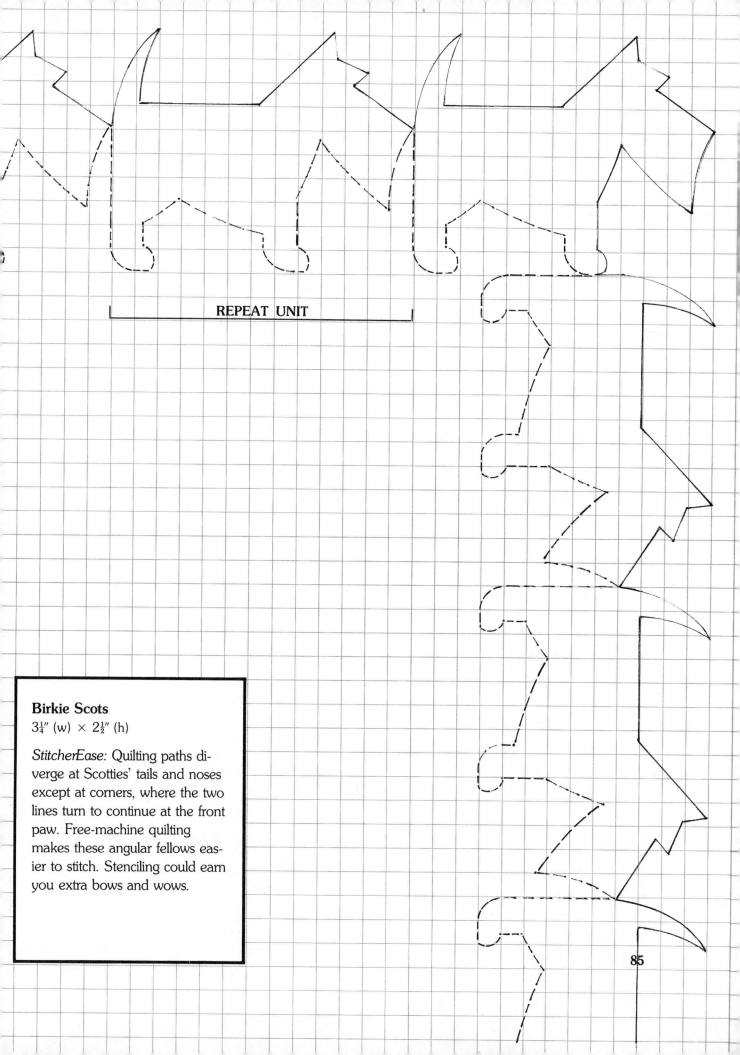

REPEAT UNIT

Birkie Scots

$3\frac{1}{4}''$ (w) $\times$ $2\frac{1}{2}''$ (h)

StitcherEase: Quilting paths diverge at Scotties' tails and noses except at corners, where the two lines turn to continue at the front paw. Free-machine quilting makes these angular fellows easier to stitch. Stenciling could earn you extra bows and wows.

85

REPEAT UNIT

With Most of My Heart
3″ (w) × 3″ (h)

StitcherEase: When using this design in rows, bring diamonds together at the end so you can quilt return trips. Quilt this design in red on white satin using the free-machine method for that special February message.

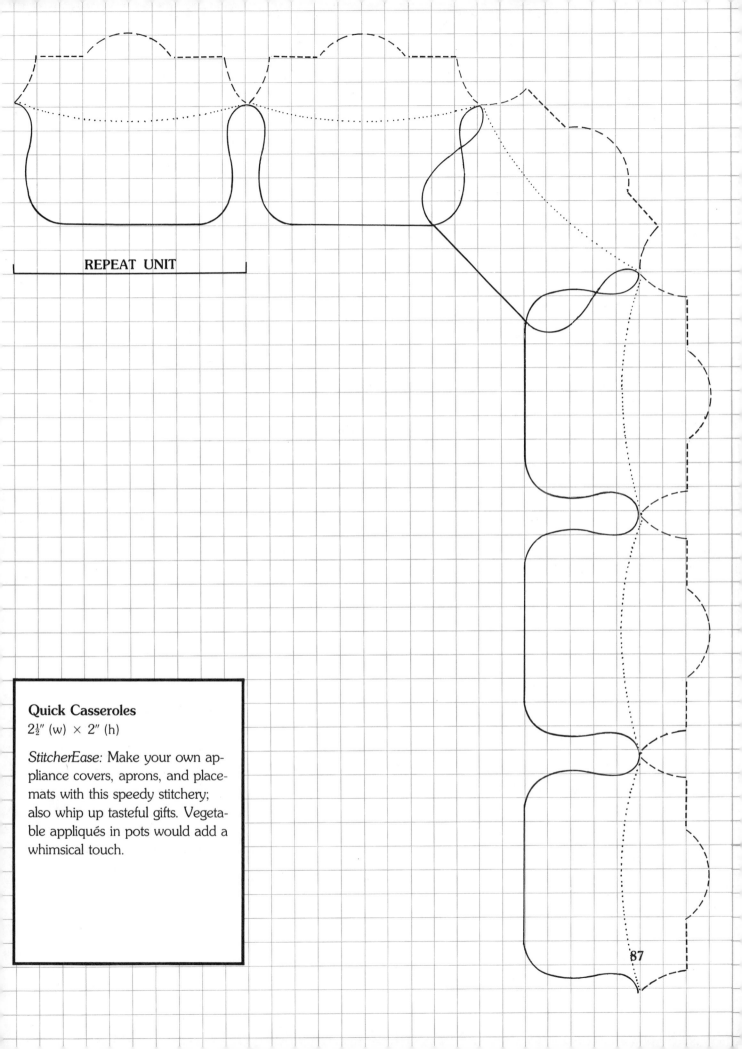

REPEAT UNIT

Quick Casseroles
$2\frac{1}{2}''$ (w) $\times$ 2″ (h)

StitcherEase: Make your own appliance covers, aprons, and placemats with this speedy stitchery; also whip up tasteful gifts. Vegetable appliqués in pots would add a whimsical touch.

87

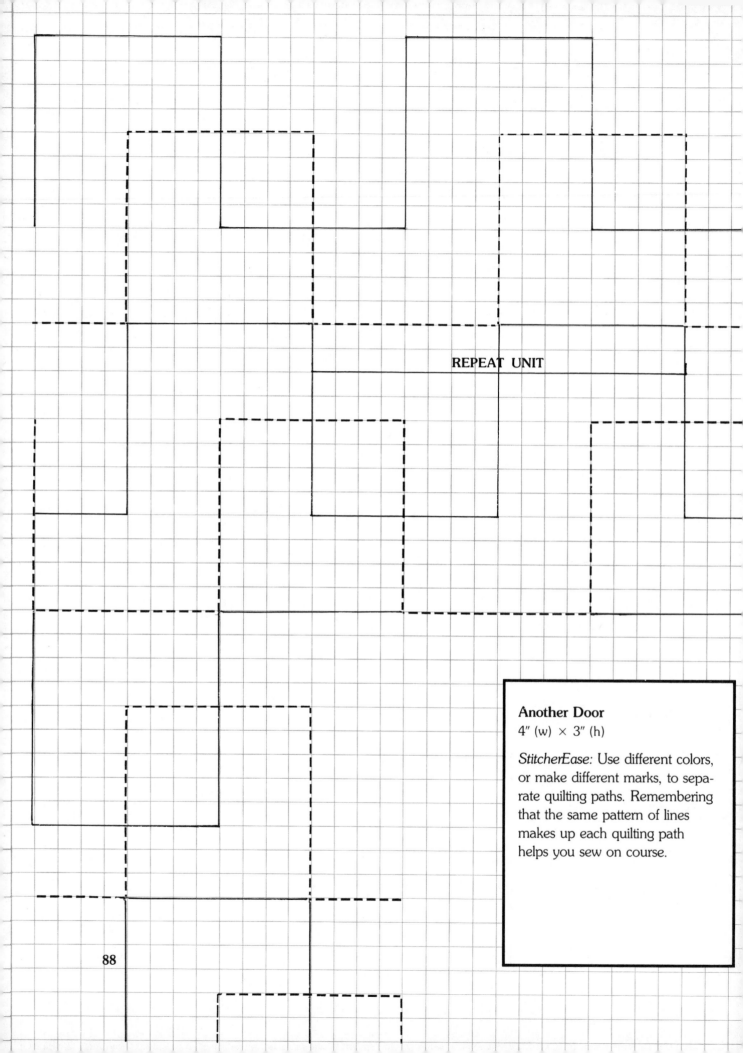

REPEAT UNIT

Another Door
4″ (w) × 3″ (h)

StitcherEase: Use different colors, or make different marks, to separate quilting paths. Remembering that the same pattern of lines makes up each quilting path helps you sew on course.

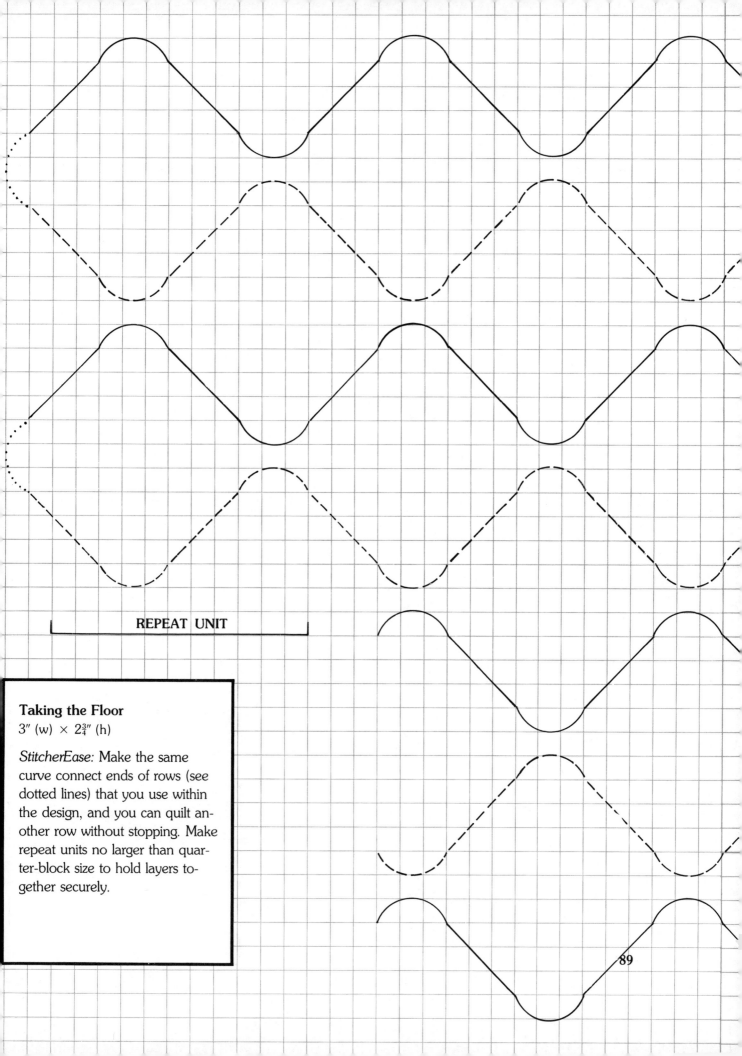

REPEAT UNIT

Taking the Floor
3″ (w) × 2¾″ (h)

StitcherEase: Make the same curve connect ends of rows (see dotted lines) that you use within the design, and you can quilt another row without stopping. Make repeat units no larger than quarter-block size to hold layers together securely.

89

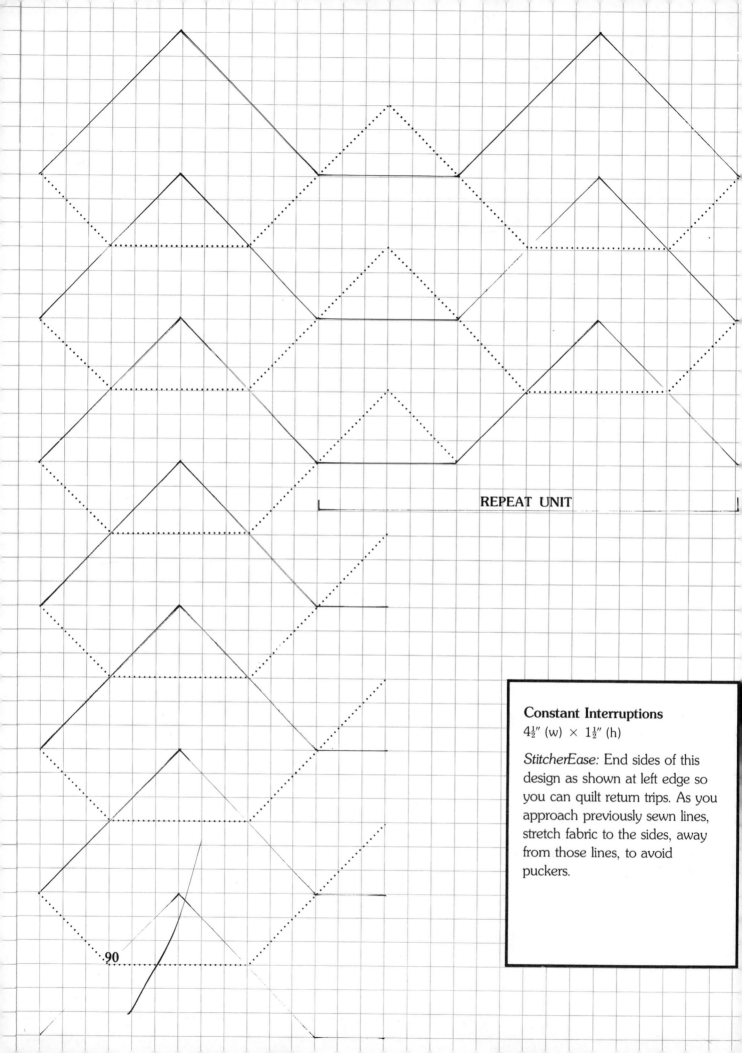

REPEAT UNIT

Constant Interruptions
$4\frac{1}{2}''$ (w) $\times$ $1\frac{1}{2}''$ (h)

StitcherEase: End sides of this
design as shown at left edge so
you can quilt return trips. As you
approach previously sewn lines,
stretch fabric to the sides, away
from those lines, to avoid
puckers.

90

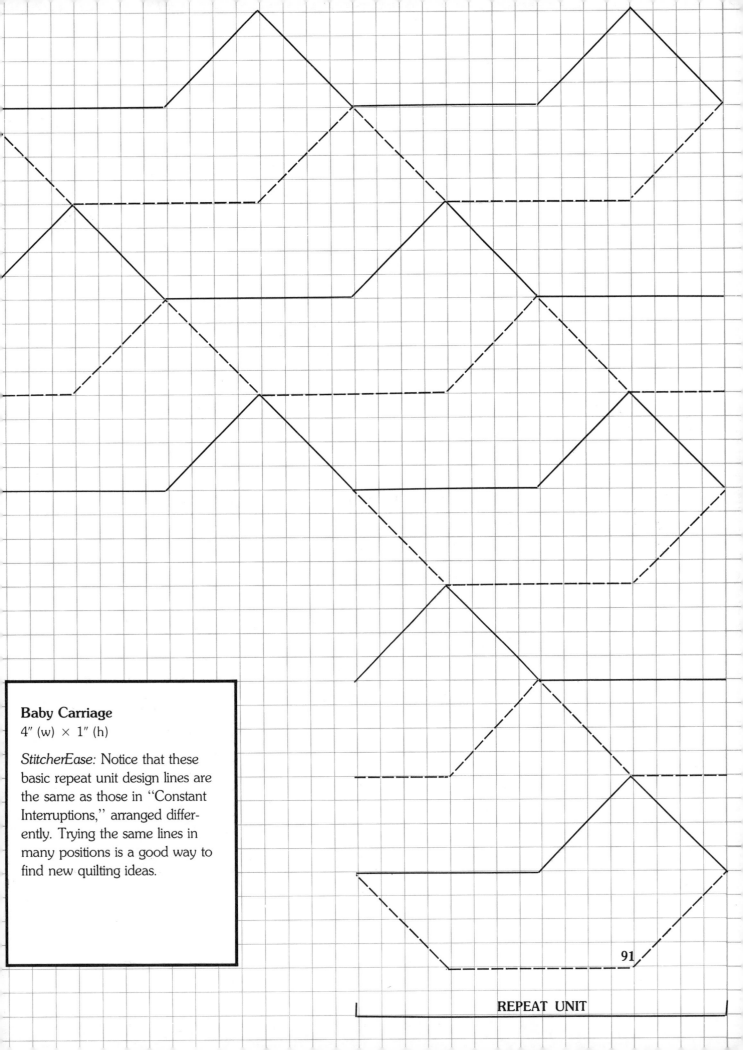

Baby Carriage
4″ (w) × 1″ (h)

StitcherEase: Notice that these basic repeat unit design lines are the same as those in "Constant Interruptions," arranged differently. Trying the same lines in many positions is a good way to find new quilting ideas.

91

REPEAT UNIT

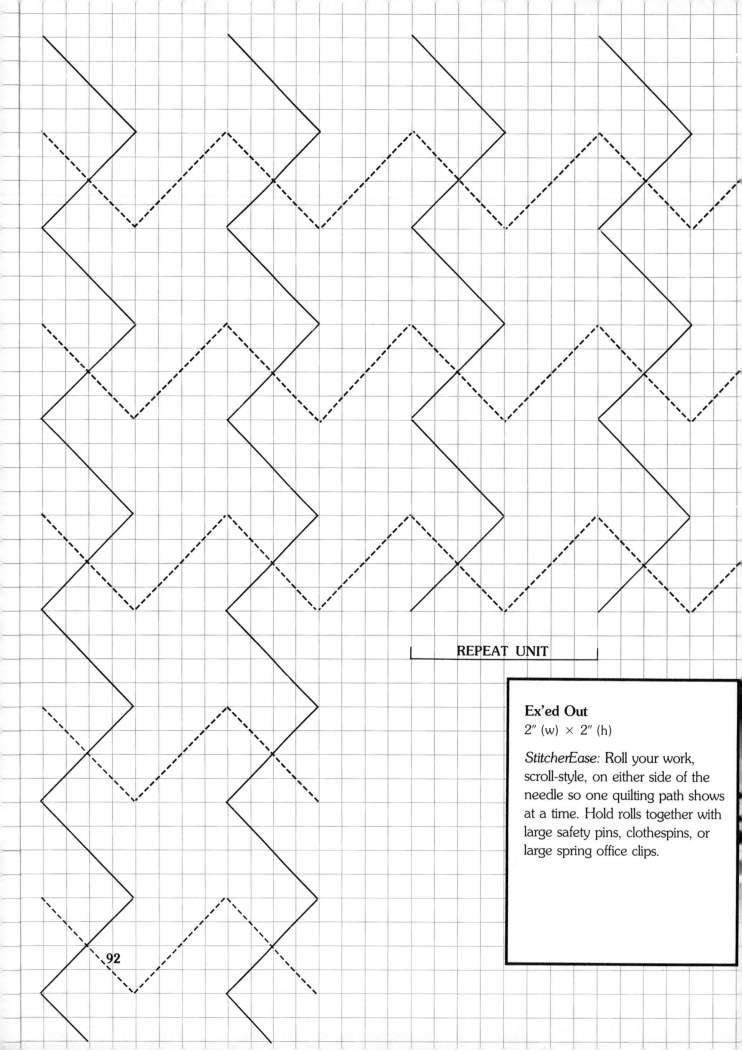

REPEAT UNIT

Ex'ed Out
2″ (w) × 2″ (h)

StitcherEase: Roll your work, scroll-style, on either side of the needle so one quilting path shows at a time. Hold rolls together with large safety pins, clothespins, or large spring office clips.

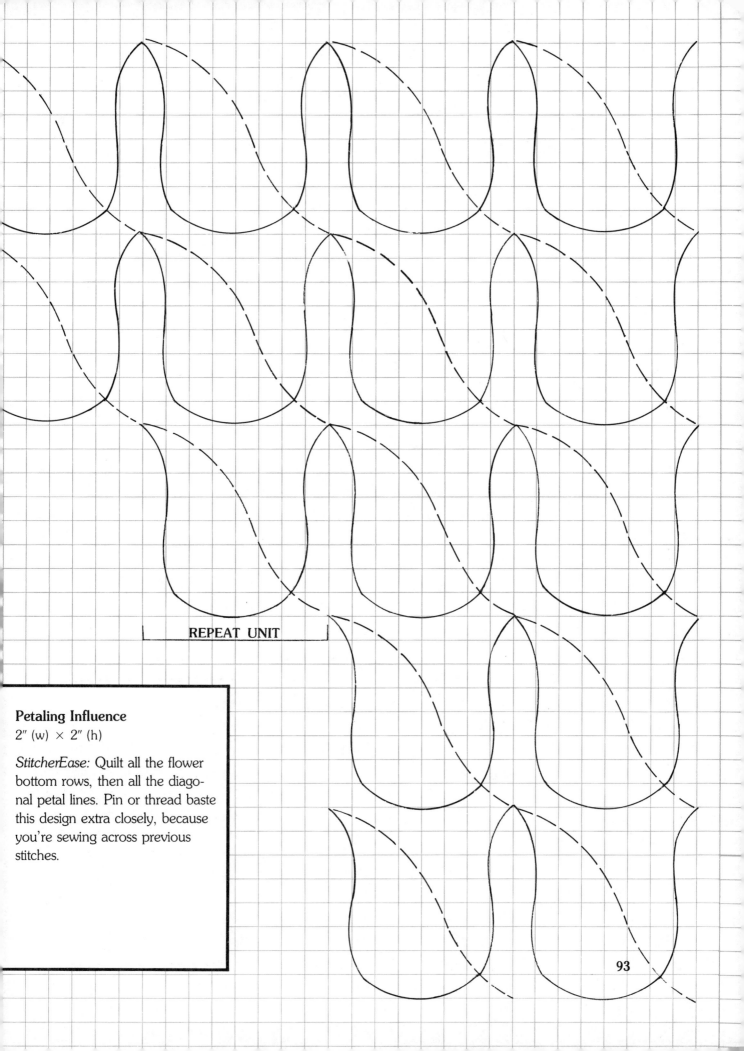

REPEAT UNIT

Petaling Influence
2″ (w) × 2″ (h)

StitcherEase: Quilt all the flower bottom rows, then all the diagonal petal lines. Pin or thread baste this design extra closely, because you're sewing across previous stitches.

93

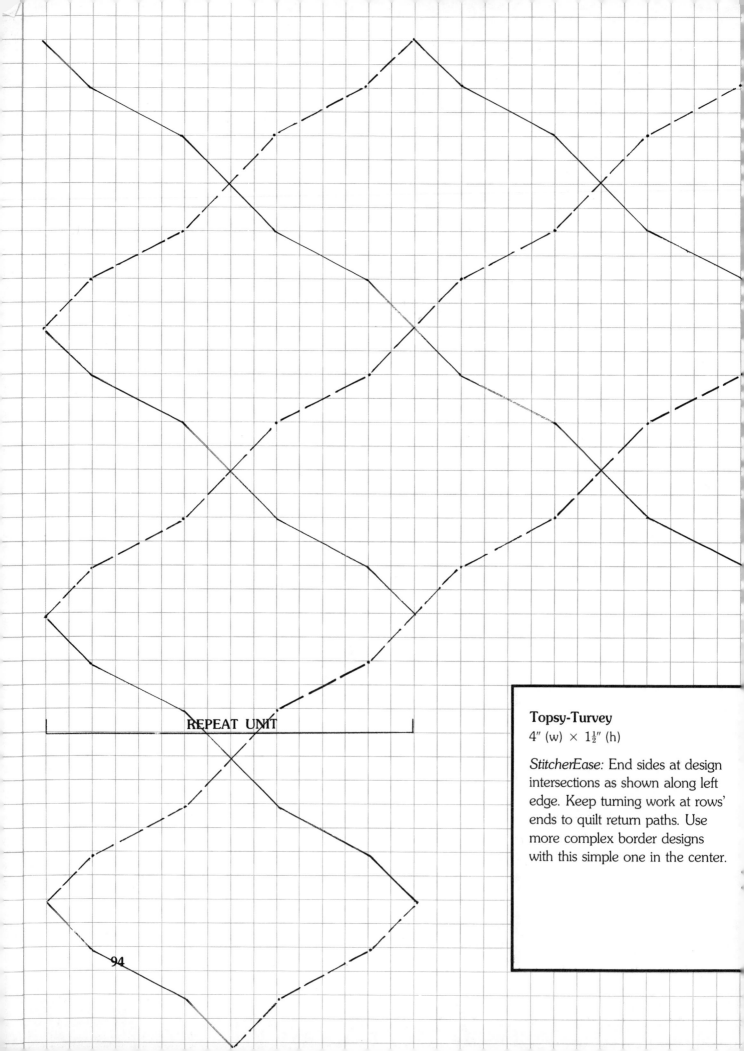

REPEAT UNIT

Topsy-Turvey
4″ (w) × 1½″ (h)

StitcherEase: End sides at design
intersections as shown along left
edge. Keep turning work at rows'
ends to quilt return paths. Use
more complex border designs
with this simple one in the center.

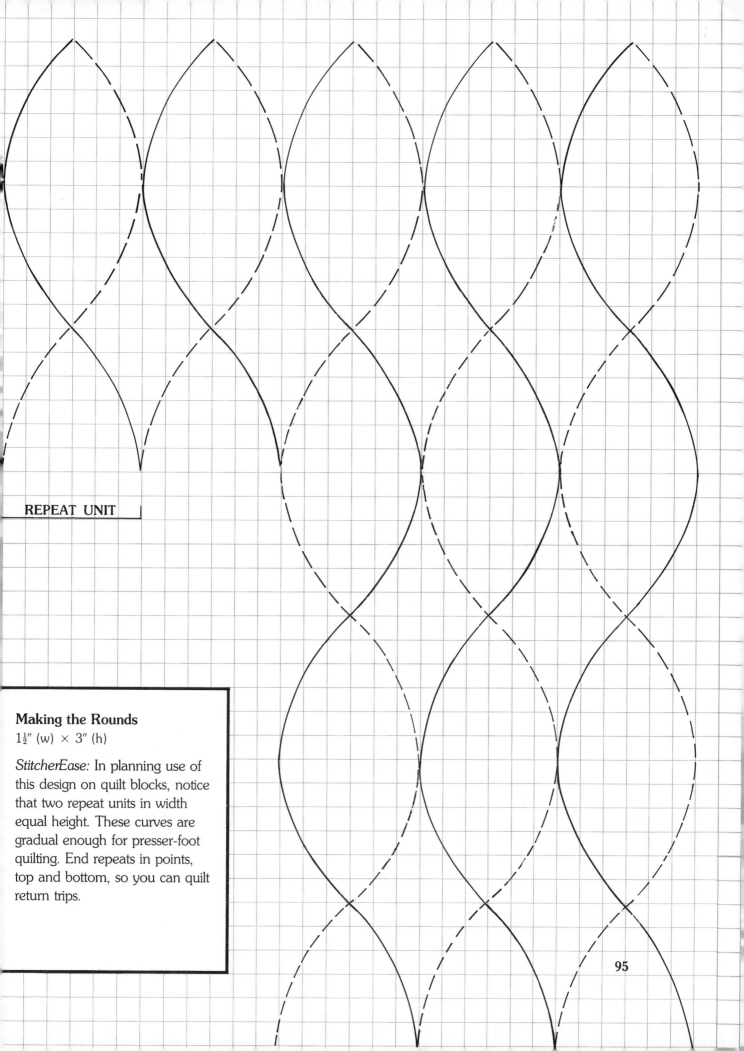

REPEAT UNIT

Making the Rounds
$1\frac{1}{2}''$ (w) × $3''$ (h)

StitcherEase: In planning use of this design on quilt blocks, notice that two repeat units in width equal height. These curves are gradual enough for presser-foot quilting. End repeats in points, top and bottom, so you can quilt return trips.

95

Shopping Center

Contact publishers and businesses for prices of publications, catalogs, and products. Be sure to enclose a self-addressed, stamped envelope for faster reply.

Publications

The Complete Book of Machine Quilting by Robbie and Tony Fanning. Chilton Book Company, Radnor, PA 19089.

Quilted Clothing by Jean Ray Laury. Oxmoor House, Inc., P. O. Box 2463, Birmingham, AL 35201.

The Artist's and Craftsman's Guide to Reducing, Enlarging and Transferring Designs by Rita Weiss. Dover Publications, Inc., 180 Varick Street, New York, NY 10014.

Open Chain. Fibar Designs, P. O. Box 2634, Menlo Park, CA 94025. (Monthly newsletter or magazine for inspiration and book reviews.)

Treadleart. 25843 Narbonne Ave., Lomita, CA 90717. (Bimonthly magazine for sewing machine art enthusiasts. Also ask for supplies catalog.)

Supply Sources

Aardvark Adventures in Handcrafts
P. O. Box 2449
Livermore, CA 94550
(415) 447-1306
   Books, embroidery thread, stampers, stencil painting supplies

The American Quilter
P. O. Box 7455
Menlo Park, CA 94025
   Stencil painting supplies, stencil plastic, quilting stencil kit (electric pen)

Cabin Fever Calicoes
5540 30th St. N.W.
Washington, DC 20015
(202) 686-0311 by 2 P.M.
   Fabrics, books, craft knives, cutting mats, Nonce marking pencils, scissors, stencil plastic, water-erasable pens

Cadillac Plastic
1400 Henderson
Fort Worth, TX 76102
(817) 332-4421
   Light box plastic, stencil plastic (for light box top, ask for White Plexiglas W-2447; for stencils, 7 ml Mylar)

Factory Outlet Buttons & Things
24 Main St., Rte. 1
Freeport, ME 04032
(207) 865-4480
   Buttons

Gohn Bros.
Box 111
Middlebury, IN 46540-0111
(219) 825-2400
   Fabrics, batting, books, safety pins, sewing thread

Home-Sew
Bethlehem, PA 18018
   Buttons, lace, trims, safety pins, scissors, sewing thread, water-erasable pens

Total Sewing, Inc.
P. O. Box 438
3729 Grand Blvd.
Brookfield, IL 60513
(312) 387-0500
   Scissors, sewing machines, parts, accessories

Treadleart
25843 Narbonne Ave.
Lomita, CA 90717
(213) 534-5122
   Books, cutting mats, Dixon Washout cloth marker, embroidery thread, Nonce marking pencils, scissors, sewing machines, parts, accessories, stampers, stencil painting supplies, stencil plastic, water-erasable pens